SPEAKING & LISTENING

A Contemporary Approach

Second Edition

SPEAKING & LISTENING

A Contemporary Approach

Second Edition

WAYNE AUSTIN SHROPE

De Anza College

Harcourt Brace Jovanovich College Publishers
Fort Worth   Philadelphia   San Diego
New York   Orlando   Austin   San Antonio
Toronto   Montreal   London   Sydney   Tokyo

Preface

While I have been pleased with the remarkable success of the first edition of *Speaking and Listening*, I have also looked forward to preparing a second edition for several reasons: (1) Students and colleagues have indicated a number of places in the book where additional explanation, definition, or example would help to clarify the activities. (2) I have been eager to replace the reprint selections at the beginning of each section with articles or speeches more attuned to the interests of today's students. (3) I wanted to add two new chapters that I have tried in my own classes and found particularly valuable.

The first of the new chapters (16) examines different kinds of communication. Though the major emphasis of the book remains on public speaking, the student is encouraged to understand and engage in other, related types of oral communication.

The second new chapter (17) discusses fact, inference, and judgment. Perhaps the most basic skills are the ability to think clearly and to communicate one's thoughts orally and in writing. Essential to these is the ability to differentiate between facts, inferences, and judgments. This chapter is designed to help students make those distinctions in both speaking and listening.

The overall aim of the book is not so much to train students in the specialized art of public speaking as to help them develop the ability to communicate. The principles described in traditional public-speaking textbooks are presented in full, but they are treated as tools for use in the context of specific communication activities.

In Chapters 1 through 11, these activities take the form of assignments, simple at first and then more complex. The purpose of the assignment format is to start students speaking immediately, to provide a specific context for all general points, and to free the instructor from the need to give detailed instructions and reminders. Step-by-step directions are given for each task, and forms for outlines and other written work are provided. The pages in the book are perforated so that the student can tear out the forms and use them during his or her presentation or can hand them in, as required.

Through the assignments the student learns chiefly by doing, building skills in a series of small steps. However, he or she also has an opportunity to learn by analyzing the work of others. A selection by a professional writer or speaker opens each of the first four parts of the book, and the student is asked at an appropriate point to reread each model and answer the discussion questions that follow it. In addition, the first nine chapters include actual student outlines and manuscripts prepared by students at De Anza College in Cupertino, California. These are samples rather than models. Guided by the discussion questions, the student is to identify the strengths and weaknesses of the samples, trying to emulate the former and avoid the latter while completing his or her own assignment.

The book can be used in various ways, depending on the time available and the emphasis of the course. If time is short, the model selections and student samples need not be discussed in class. Assignments can also be omitted at the instructor's discretion, and Chapters 12 through 19, which do not follow the assignment format, offer additional flexibility. For example, if listening is an important concern of the course, Chapters 12 and 13 should be assigned early in the term, and students should set up a listening notebook as instructed in Chapter 13. If listening is less important, those chapters can be read outside class or even eliminated altogether.

Virtually the only feature of the book that is not susceptible to adjustment is its stress on communication as a highly personal type of behavior. The student is told, directly and indirectly, that his or her own history and personality are unique, that what is unique is interesting to others, and that communicating well requires self-revelation as well as technical facility. Students are urged to be open and honest about their own thoughts and feelings, and to listen not only to what others say but to what they mean. This type of communication, which shows the influence of encounter groups and sensitivity training, may not be easy, but it can be one of the most enjoyable and rewarding experiences that life has to offer.

I wish to express my appreciation to my wife, Ruby Shrope, for her invaluable assistance and encouragement in the preparation of the manuscript for this book, and to Paul Roman, Lory Frohbach, and Faye Steiger, who supplied the sample student manuscripts and outlines.

Wayne Austin Shrope

Contents

4 Communicating to Solve Problems

5 Listening

6 Improving Oral Communication

1
COMMUNICATING FOR ENJOYMENT

Wherever people go and whatever they do, their greatest pleasure is often talking with other people. At a party or a picnic, a social hall or a private home, what people seem to enjoy most is the companionship of others. They enjoy companionship because of the close relationship that comes when people share themselves with others—their inner thoughts and hopes, their aspirations and dreams, their present experiences and those that they treasure from the past.

Your first experiences in this course will call upon you to share these things with your classmates. Doing this well will require you to sharpen your memory, your perceptions, and your imagination. Your immediate rewards will be a greater understanding of yourself, a greater enjoyment of the things you do now and have done in the past, and a closer personal relationship with the members of your class.

from UNIVERSITY DAYS

James Thurber

This selection, in which the noted humorist James Thurber re-
counts incidents from his experiences as a student at the Ohio State
University, is similar in purpose, organization, and development to
the assignments you will be given in Part 1. Give it a first reading
now. Later on, you will be asked to reread it and to analyze it, using
the discussion questions that follow the story, in order to help you
understand the assignments in Part 1 and to improve your own
communication.

I passed all the other courses that I took at my University,
but I could never pass botany. This was because all botany
students had to spend several hours a week in a laboratory
looking through a microscope at plant cells, and I could never
see through a microscope. I never once saw a cell through a
microscope. This used to enrage my instructor. He would wander around the laboratory pleased with the progress all the
students were making in drawing the involved and, so I am
told, interesting structure of flower cells, until he came to me. I
would just be standing there. "I can't see anything," I would
say. He would begin patiently enough, explaining how anybody can see through a microscope, but he would always end
up in a fury, claiming that I could *too* see through a microscope
but just pretended that I couldn't. "It takes away from the
beauty of flowers anyway," I used to tell him. "We are not
concerned with beauty in this course," he would say. "We are
concerned solely with what I may call the *mechanics* of flars."
"Well," I'd say, "I can't see anything." "Try it just once again,"
he'd say, and I would put my eye to the microscope and see
nothing at all, except now and again a nebulous milky
substance—a phenomenon of maladjustment. You were supposed to see a vivid, restless clockwork of sharply defined plant
cells. "I see what looks like a lot of milk," I would tell him.
This, he claimed, was the result of my not having adjusted the

microscope properly, so he would readjust it for me, or rather, for himself. And I would look again and see milk.

I finally took a deferred pass, as they called it, and waited a year and tried again. (You had to pass one of the biological sciences or you couldn't graduate.) The professor had come back from vacation brown as a berry, bright-eyed and eager to explain cell-structure again to his classes. "Well," he said to me, cheerily, when we met in the first laboratory hour of the semester, "we're going to see cells this time, aren't we?" "Yes, sir," I said. Students to right of me and to left of me and in front of me were seeing cells; what's more, they were quietly drawing pictures of them in their notebooks. Of course, I didn't see anything.

"We'll try it," the professor said to me, grimly, "with every adjustment of the microscope known to man. As God is my witness, I'll arrange this glass so that you see cells through it or I'll give up teaching. In twenty-two years of botany, I—" He cut off abruptly for he was beginning to quiver all over, like Lionel Barrymore, and he genuinely wished to hold onto his temper; his scenes with me had taken a great deal out of him.

So we tried it with every adjustment of the microscope known to man. With only one of them did I see anything but blackness or the familiar lacteal opacity, and that time I saw, to my pleasure and amazement, a variegated constellation of flecks, specks, and dots. These I hastily drew. The instructor, noting my activity, came back from an adjoining desk, a smile on his lips and his eyebrows high in hope. He looked at my cell drawing. "What's that?" he demanded, with a hint of a squeal in his voice. "That's what I saw," I said. "You didn't, you didn't, you *didn't!*" he screamed, losing control of his temper instantly, and he bent over and squinted into the microscope. His head snapped up. "That's your eye!" he shouted. "You've fixed the lens so that it reflects! You've drawn your eye!"

Another course that I didn't like, but somehow managed to pass, was economics. I went to that class straight from the botany class, which didn't help me any in understanding either subject. I used to get them mixed up. But not as mixed up as another student in my economics class who came there direct from a physics laboratory. He was a tackle on the football team, named Bolenciecwcz. At that time Ohio State University had one of the best football teams in the country, and Bolenciecwcz was one of its outstanding stars. In order to be eligible to play it was necessary for him to keep up in his studies, a very difficult matter, for while he was not dumber than an ox he was not any smarter. Most of his professors were lenient and helped him along. None gave him more hints, in answering questions, or asked him simpler ones than the economics professor, a thin, timid man named Bassum. One day when we were on the subject of transportation and distribution, it came Bolenciecwcz's turn to answer a question. "Name one means of transportation," the professor said to him. No light came into the big tackle's eyes. "Just any means of transportation," said the professor. Bolenciecwcz sat staring at him. "That is," pursued the professor, "any medium, agency, or method of going from one place to another." Bolenciecwcz had the look of a man who is being led into a trap. "You may choose among steam, horse-drawn, or electrically propelled vehicles," said the instructor. "I might suggest the one which we commonly take in making long journeys across land." There was a profound silence in which everybody stirred uneasily, including Bolenciecwcz and Mr. Bassum. Mr. Bassum abruptly broke this silence in an amazing manner. "Choo-choo-choo," he said, in a low voice, and turned instantly scarlet. He glanced appealingly around the room. All of us, of course, shared Mr. Bassum's desire that Bolenciecwcz should stay abreast of the class in economics, for the Illinois game, one of the hardest and most important of the season, was only a week off. "Toot, toot, too-tooooooot!" some student with a deep voice moaned, and we all looked encouragingly at Bolenciecwcz. Somebody else gave a fine imitation of a locomotive letting off steam. Mr. Bassum himself rounded off the little show. "Ding, dong, ding, dong," he said, hopefully. Bolenciecwcz was staring at the floor now, trying to think, his great brow furrowed, his huge hands rubbing together, his face red.

"How did you come to college this year, Mr. Bolenciecwcz?" asked the professor. "*Chuffa* chuffa, *chuffa* chuffa."

"M'father sent me," said the football player.

"What on?" asked Bassum.

"I git an 'lowance," said the tackle, in a low husky voice, obviously embarrassed.

"No, no," said Bassum. "Name a means of transportation. What did you *ride* here on?"

"Train," said Bolenciecwcz.

"Quite right," said the professor. "Now, Mr. Nugent, will you tell us—" . . .

Ohio State was a land grant university and therefore two years of military drill was compulsory. We drilled with old Springfield rifles and studied the tactics of the Civil War even though the World War was going on at the time. At 11 o'clock each morning thousands of freshmen and sophomores used to deploy over the campus, moodily creeping up on the old chemistry building. It was good training for the kind of warfare that was waged at Shiloh but it had no connection with what was going on in Europe. Some people used to think there was German money behind it, but they didn't dare say so or they would have been thrown in jail as German spies. It was a period of muddy thought and marked, I believe, the decline of higher education in the Middle West.

As a soldier I was never any good at all. Most of the cadets were glumly indifferent soldiers, but I was no good at all. Once General Littlefield, who was commandant of the cadet corps, popped up in front of me during regimental drill and snapped,

"You are the main trouble with this university!" I think he meant that my type was the main trouble with the university but he may have meant me individually. I was mediocre at drill, certainly—that is, until my senior year. By that time I had drilled longer than anybody else in the Western Conference, having failed at military at the end of each preceding year so that I had to do it all over again. I was the only senior still in uniform. The uniform which, when new, had made me look like an interurban railway conductor, now that it had become faded and too tight made me look like Bert Williams in his bellboy act. This had a definitely bad effect on my morale. Even so, I had become by sheer practice little short of wonderful at squad maneuvers.

One day General Littlefield picked our company out of the whole regiment and tried to get it mixed up by putting it through one movement after another as fast as we could execute them: squads right, squads left, squads on right into line, squads right about, squads left front into line, etc. In about three minutes one hundred and nine men were marching in one direction and I was marching away from them at an angle of forty degrees, all alone. "Company, halt!" shouted General Littlefield. "That man is the only man who has it right!" I was made a corporal for my achievement.

The next day General Littlefield summoned me to his office. He was swatting flies when I went in. I was silent and he was silent too, for a long time. I don't think he remembered me or why he had sent for me, but he didn't want to admit it. He swatted some more flies, keeping his eyes on them narrowly before he let go with the swatter. "Button up your coat!" he snapped. Looking back on it now I can see that he meant me although he was looking at a fly, but I just stood there. Another fly came to rest on a paper in front of the general and began rubbing its hind legs together. The general lifted the swatter cautiously. I moved restlessly and the fly flew away. "You startled him!" barked General Littlefield, looking at me severely. I said I was sorry. "That won't help the situation!" snapped the General, with cold military logic. I didn't see what I could do except offer to chase some more flies toward his desk, but I didn't say anything. He stared out the window at the faraway figures of co-eds crossing the campus toward the library. Finally, he told me I could go. So I went. He either didn't know which cadet I was or else he forgot what he wanted to see me about. It may have been that he wished to apologize for having called me the main trouble with the university; or maybe he had decided to compliment me on my brilliant drilling of the day before and then at the last minute decided not to. I don't know. I don't think about it much any more.

QUESTIONS FOR DISCUSSION

(to be answered after you have read Chapters 1 and 2)

1. This story involves three incidents. What gives it unity?

2. How much of the first incident is introduction? Where does the rising action begin? Where is the climax?

3. Where is the climax of the second incident?

4. How are the three incidents developed? Which do you find more effective? Why?

5. What makes the last line effective?

6. What are the elements of Thurber's style of humor?

7. Can you remember any humorous or unusual experiences you have had in school?

8. Can you remember any humorous incidents involving minor conflicts like those in the selection?

1
INTRODUCING YOURSELF

It seems appropriate to begin your communication experiences by getting acquainted with the other members of your class. Of course, the speaker-audience situation does not allow the give-and-take that conversation does, but the basic principle is the same: you must communicate yourself. To do that, you need to give your listeners more than just objective facts about yourself. They also need to know what you think and how you feel. When you mention a place you have lived, describe the personal things you remember—things no one but you may have noticed or felt. When you mention something you like or dislike, give your personal reasons for feeling that way, frankly and honestly. Tell about the things you do well, but confess your inadequacies too.

When others do these things, notice how quickly you begin to feel that you know them and can empathize with them. You don't have to know some people long to know them well, if they express themselves honestly and openly. Learning to do this, and to respond to it in others, can significantly improve your ability in conversation, especially when meeting people for the first time.

Learn the names of the members of your class as rapidly as possible. Try to develop the feeling that you're all friends and that your purpose is to help each other. No one should ever feel that he or she is alone in front of an audience or that his or her audience is a hostile enemy. Audiences as a whole, inside and outside the classroom, are really very appreciative and forgiving. If the class develops a friendly, relaxed atmosphere, each person will learn more and teach more to others—and enjoy doing it!

Don't allow yourself to become overly critical, only looking for faults in the presentations of others. Fault-finding requires little talent or intelligence. Instead, try to point out what other speakers do that is good (they need reminding just as you do) and how they could improve what is less good. Both these steps are harder than fault-finding, and much more constructive.

ASSIGNMENT

Spend some time thinking about yourself. Be very honest with yourself about who you are and what you are. What are your hopes and ambitions? Do you want to travel? Do you want to get married and raise a family? Do you plan to go into a trade, a profession, or a business? What is there about you that may suit you for these activities? What are your likes and dislikes? Do you like art, music, blond hair, swimming pools, sunsets, parties? What are your strengths and weaknesses? Do you think you are good at science and math but poor in English and speech? Do you think you are good at analyzing an essay but poor at understanding how an automobile works? What experiences have you had that have caused you to feel this way about yourself? Were you successful in teaching Sunday school and unsuccessful in writing essays? Did a close relationship with your father develop your interest in football? Did your admiration for a particular actor cause you to become interested in drama?

Select the things about you that seem most significant and organize them into an oral presentation for your class. In a friendly, conversational, and intensely personal way, "chat" with your classmates about your background, your interests, and your plans for the future.

PURPOSES

1. To help you understand and communicate yourself.

2. To acquaint you with your class and to establish a friendly, cooperative atmosphere.

3. To make your first time in front of the class as relaxed as possible. After all, you are the world's leading authority on your topic, so talking about it should be easy. Remember that people are interested in people, and they will be interested in you if you let them.

4. To give you practice in using the pronoun I honestly and modestly. It is frequently said that speakers should not use I because it seems egotistical, but no one has ever objected to the use of I in sentences like "How much do I owe you?" and "I like the way you did that." The important thing is how you use I. You can talk about your successes and your strengths without seeming immodest if you also admit your inadequacies and show your appreciation and admiration for the abilities and successes of other people.

DEVELOPMENT

Try using a chronological (time-order) pattern for your organization. Begin with the past, bring yourself up to the present, and project yourself into the future.

1.   Give your audience a brief biographical sketch: when and where you were born, where you've been, what you've done, and so forth.

2.   Tell something about your current situation: married or single? living at home or in your own apartment? employed? full-time student?

3.   Tell about your hobbies and special interests. These give real insight into your personality.

4.   Talk about your ambitions and plans for the future. Be sure always to give your personal feelings and reactions to the things you mention. This information will not only help your class get to know you but help them be more helpful to you when they discuss your future assignments.

PRACTICE

Write down in very brief outline form some of the things you plan to cover. You can develop your outline using three main headings: past, present, and future. This outline is for your use only, so it needn't be too detailed—just write down some key words under each of the three main headings to remind yourself of the essential material in your presentation.

Working from this outline, rehearse your speech aloud. Keep your delivery as conversational and natural as possible. Listen to yourself to be sure that you are using your own natural vocal inflections. Watch yourself in the mirror to be sure that you are using your own natural gestures and facial expressions.

To keep your delivery spontaneous, allow what you say to develop and change as you rehearse. If mentioning someplace you have lived makes a picture flash through your mind or causes an emotional reaction, include that in your speech. If you mention something that you like or don't like, explain why. If you get too many of these reactions, sort them out as you rehearse and include in your final speech only the ones that you, personally, remember as the most vivid or most important ones.

Keep rehearsing until you feel that you know what you're going to say and how you're going to say it, and until you feel that you are giving the facts and impressions that will best communicate to your listeners what you are like.

DELIVERY

When you deliver your speech to your audience, maintain the natural and spontaneous delivery patterns you have achieved in your practice.

11

Look at every member of your audience before you start talking, and maintain good eye contact with them throughout your speech.

Keep your manner enthusiastic and friendly throughout. Show your audience the same eagerness to communicate that you show in animated conversation with your closest friends. Keep your energy up. You must project not only your words but your personality to every member of your audience. After you have finished, you should feel at least a little tired, both physically and emotionally. If you don't, you probably haven't really given of yourself to your audience.

EVALUATION

To keep this first assignment as relaxed and informal as possible, no outline is required and no grade will be given. But, of course, the instructor and the members of your class will form some definite opinions about you on the basis of what you say and how you say it. They may also form inferences on the basis of what you don't say!

Notice as you listen to others in your class how you make judgments about them. What qualities in them do you admire, and how do they project these qualities? While you are listening, fill out the listening forms as described in Chapter 13, which will help you get to know the other members of your class as individuals. After you have heard all the introductory speeches, fill in the audience analysis form given on pages 271–73, which will help you get to know your audience as a group.

2
TELLING YOUR EXPERIENCE FOR ENJOYMENT

One characteristic of good conversationalists is their ability to tell stories well—stories about their experiences, observations about books they have read and movies they have seen, and so on. It seems that the funniest, most exciting, most wonderful things happen to these people. They really enjoy living!

But listen carefully. It's not that more exciting things happen to these persons; it's just that they tell them better. Examine your own experience. Things that others would enjoy hearing about happen to you every day. They don't have to be earth-shattering in importance. Stand-up comedians are professional (and often very well paid) storytellers, and what do *they* talk about? Their homes, their wives or husbands, their kids, their mothers-in-law, their dogs . . . .

Improve your ability to tell stories and you'll improve your conversational ability and your personality. A good storyteller is welcome in any group.

ASSIGNMENT

Think over some of the funny, embarrassing, and frightening things that have happened to you during your life. Remember the time you ran the wrong way in a basketball game, the time you forgot your lines on stage, the time you thought a burglar was trying to break into your house. Think especially about experiences that you have already described to friends. Which stories did they most enjoy hearing about? Select one of these to tell to your class.

PRELIMINARY ORGANIZATION

Limit yourself to one very specific experience so that you can tell about it in detail. Instead of describing your weekend at Yosemite, tell about the night a bear wandered into your camp.

In remembering your experience, exercise your imagination. Recreate for yourself in vivid detail how things looked, sounded, smelled, and felt. Remember how other people looked and what they said, and try to remember all the things you thought and felt during the experience. Then begin selecting the details that will best help your listeners to visualize and share your experience.

Your story will need to have a clear beginning, middle, and end. Most stories have a three-part structure: exposition, rising action and climax, and conclusion. Each part has important functions, so each must be planned carefully.

Your first task is to get the attention of your listeners. The beginning of your story should arouse enough curiosity to hold their attention through the exposition, whose major function is to give your listeners whatever background information they need to understand and enjoy the story. You must present the characters, describe the setting, give the time, and make the situation clear. The situation usually involves a central character who is trying to do something and another character (or force) who is preventing him or her from doing it, or trying to. This conflict is the basis of the story.

When you have made the conflict clear, the rising action of the story begins. This middle section should be the longest part, because it includes all or almost all of the action. It consists of a series of events, usually in chronological order, which leads to a climax. The climax is the highest point in action and suspense, probably the part of the story that made you decide to tell it.

After the climax you should plan a conclusion for your story. The ending should answer any questions your listeners might have about the fate of the characters. It should also be as short as possible, because an audience's attention declines very rapidly after the climax.

DEVELOPMENT

After you have blocked out the basic organization of your story, go back over each part and plan the development in detail.

EXPOSITION

The opening of your story should be forceful. Avoid limp openings like these:

One summer afternoon my parents, my girl friend, her two younger sisters, and I took a trip to San Francisco.

In the summer of 1963 I spent a lot of time looking for a new car.

Find imaginative openings like these:

I lay on the ready line waiting for the range officer to give the signal to raise the targets. If I could do as well as I had yesterday and the day before, I knew I would qualify as an expert rifleman. I had finished the slow-fire positions and rapid-fire-in-prone-position, and scored well. As I waited for the signal to start my last turn, rapid-fire-in-kneeling-position, I wasn't even worried . . . .

In a few minutes we would meet the other team on the field. Warm-up was over, and the coach was giving us last-minute instructions and a pep talk to help knock out the butterflies. It was my first college football game. I noticed that my palms were sweating . . . .

All I said was, "Sure, I'll try surfing." How was I to know that my new friend's favorite beach was called "The Cataract" for a very good reason? I had only arrived in Hawaii that afternoon . . . .

These openings are particularly effective because they establish a conflict immediately. In the first one, the central character is trying to qualify as an expert marksman but may be prevented from achieving his goal by his own overconfidence. In the second opening, two conflicts are introduced, the first between two football teams and the second between the central character and his own nervousness. In the third, a conflict between the speaker and "The Cataract" is foreshadowed.

Now that you have decided how to capture your listeners' attention, plan vivid descriptions of the characters and the setting. The audience needs concrete details in order to visualize the characters and the situation in their own minds. For example: He was a wizened little man, and his brown, double-breasted suit looked at least two sizes too big for him. There was a gravy stain on his tie. I noticed that his hands were trembling.

Many stories have less impact than they should because the storyteller fails to give enough information for the listener to see the characters and share their feelings.

RISING ACTION

In the middle section of your story, continue to use vivid descriptions and vivid action words: *raced, flopped, dragged, sauntered, bawled, screamed, whispered.* Recall every detail of your experience, more than you can possibly use, so that you can select the best details. If your memory falters, use your imagination to reconstruct how things must have been and what people must have said. Don't hesitate to exaggerate some of the details. This will give the story the larger-than-life quality that is found in most literature, and it will help you hold attention and get the response you want.

Create suspense in the rising action of your story by making the central character and his or her antagonist as equal in strength as possible, so that the audience won't know in advance how the story is going to turn out. In the examples of imaginative openings given above, specific descriptions of the central character's overconfidence or lack of confidence, of the ability or power of the opposing team, and of the surfing conditions at "The Cataract" would help develop conflict and suspense.

Two other devices that create suspense are setbacks and dilemmas. A setback occurs when, after the central character has decided how to reach his or her goal, the plan goes awry so that he or she must formulate a new one. A dilemma occurs when the central character must choose between two equally unpleasant alternatives. As you describe setbacks and dilemmas, tell your listeners what went on in the mind of your central character when he or she confronted each problem.

Use devices like these to build suspense up to the climax. Be sure to identify the climax clearly in your own mind. It is the moment of greatest suspense and highest interest, and it should occur just before the resolution of the story. In fact, if you can, you should plan the story so that it ends at the climax.

A particularly effective method of developing characters and emotions is the use of dialogue. Telling a story well is partly an acting job. Say what the characters said, and say it the way they said it—including nonverbal elements like gestures and facial expressions. You may not remember exactly what people said, but you know the kinds of people they were and can imagine what they probably said. This method of re-creating dialogue is commonly used by writers. (Notice how effectively James Thurber has used this technique in the selection beginning on page 3 of this text.)

CONCLUSION

Make the conclusion as brief as possible. If you must include some information after the climax, use the bare essentials. The effect of a story can be destroyed if it drags on and on after the climax. But don't leave your audience hanging. They will want to know how the events turned out and what happened to the characters, if it was not made clear before the climax. To select the necessary information for the ending, put yourself in your listeners' place. If you were hearing the story for the first time, what additional information would you want?

At this point it would be helpful to analyze the James Thurber story that begins on page 3 and the sample manuscript that begins on page 19.

Discussion questions are included to assist in your analysis of each.

Now make two copies of the outline for your own story, on the forms provided on pages 21–28. Give one outline to your instructor, with the blank evaluation form provided for his or her use (page 29), and keep the other outline for your own use in practicing and delivering your story.

PRACTICE

As in the last assignment, practice your story aloud several times, listening to yourself and watching yourself in the mirror. Keep your delivery spontaneous, natural, and energetic. Use gestures and dialogue wherever possible, to make the characters real for your audience.

If the story is humorous, use exaggeration not only in your descriptions but in your delivery as well. Use large gestures, facial expressions, and vocal inflections, especially when telling what you thought, what people said, and what they did. The right degree of exaggeration will assure you the laughs you want. Show a great deal of enthusiasm and energy, so that the audience knows you relish this opportunity to share your experience with them.

If the story is serious, use a more restricted, objective style of delivery. Allow the many specific details in your material to convey its emotional impact. If you seem to be intensely reliving pain, sorrow, or fear, the audience may be distracted by your present emotional state and unable to concentrate on the story itself. A more objective, subtle style makes the emotional content of the story clearer because it stands out in bold relief from the objectivity of your delivery.

Continue practicing until you feel that you have the material and delivery under control and can present the story with confidence.

DELIVERY

Follow the suggestions given in your previous assignment, and in addition, give some thought to your posture. Stand with your weight evenly distributed on both feet. Don't be stiff, but use an alert, erect posture rather than a limp, dull one. There is a high correlation between a speaker's posture and audience attention.

CRITICISM

With this assignment, members of the class should begin offering each other helpful suggestions. They may be given in class or outside class, formally or informally. The important thing is that they be given in a positive and constructive way. First tell another speaker what parts of his material and delivery you thought *were* effective; then point out

17

specifically how the presentation might have been improved. Tell him what additions, deletions, or changes would have helped you, as a member of the audience, understand and appreciate more fully the experience described in the story. To assist you in doing this, use the listening forms described in Chapter 13 to take notes on your classmates' talks.

Criticize your own presentation in a similar way. If you achieved the effect you wanted, ask yourself why. If you did not, try to determine what you could have done that would have been more successful. The presentations of other members of the class should offer you some excellent ideas about how to improve your own work. When you receive suggestions from your instructor and other class members, compare them with your self-criticisms. Then make a composite list of your strengths and weaknesses, for use in future assignments.

SAMPLE STUDENT MANUSCRIPT

This sample manuscript and the sample manuscripts and outlines in later chapters were submitted by students at De Anza Community College in Cupertino, California. It is important that you read them as examples of student work, not as models. They have clear strengths, but they have weaknesses as well.

After you have analyzed the sample manuscript, compare the material in the story you are planning to give with the material in this story. Can you develop similar strengths? Can you avoid similar weaknesses? (You should make an outline of your speech rather than prepare a manuscript. The manuscript has been included here to facilitate fuller discussion.)

(1)   The day came in 1953. It grew very dark outside. The trees were blowing, and the houses were shaking. All of a sudden it began to rain. It rained and thundered, and lightning broke out in the sky. We heard on the radio that a tornado was coming through our little town of Baldwin, Kansas.

(2)   My father was away, and we had just moved into a very old farmhouse. The past owner said there was a cellar approximately ten feet from the back door. So away we went, dog and all, into the cellar. My brother and I had our flannel pajamas on; my mother was still dressed. Through our fright, it was lucky she remembered to bring a blanket and candle.

(3)   I had never been in the cellar before, and as I looked around me I saw blank concrete walls. We had no time to clean, though the floor was dirty and there were cobwebs in the corners. The furniture consisted of one small army cot and a nightstand. The smell was very musty, as the cellar was damp and had no ventilation. Also, to make things worse, there was a frog in the corner croaking every two minutes.

(4)   The peril grew as the three of us sat snuggled up on the little cot. We could still hear the wind, rain, thunder, and lightning. Would it ever go away? Where is my father? Is our house still there? Are my rabbits blown away? I hope the school isn't there. These things were in my mind, even though my mother tried to keep us singing and happy. But all I could hear was the wind and the croaking of the frog.

(5)   The night seemed like an eternity.

(6)   As we woke up from our limited sleep, there was no rain. As we listened harder we could hear no wind either. My brave brother, acting like the man of the house, carefully opened the cellar doors. Thoughts ran through my head. Would we be the only ones alive? Is our house still there? My mother and I slowly walked up the stairs. It was so quiet and still; it was like a dream.

(7)   As we looked around we were amazed. Our house was still there! The barn was there. Our rabbit cage was still there but turned over. As we looked down the road, we could see our neighbor's house, and we knew they were all right.

(8) Later, on the radio, we heard that the tornado had bypassed the town of Baldwin. I needn't tell you how thankful we were.

(9) That coming Sunday the church was filled to the brim, and no matter how hard I prayed the schoolhouse was still there.

QUESTIONS FOR DISCUSSION

1. How does the opening arouse curiosity?

2. Where does the exposition end and the rising action begin?

3. What details in the beginning are particularly effective? What important details have been omitted?

4. Where is the climax?

5. What details in the ending are particularly effective?

6. Are the questions in paragraphs 4 and 6 effective? In what way?

7. What is the purpose of the last sentence in the story?

8. One of the greatest problems in this story is faulty connection and subordination of ideas. For example, the author uses the connective as seven times. Try rewriting some of these sentences to give variety in connecting words and to show the relationship of the ideas more clearly.

9. Find other examples of faulty connection and subordination of ideas and try rewriting them.

OUTLINE: TELLING YOUR EXPERIENCE FOR ENJOYMENT

EXPOSITION

1 Statement to arouse curiosity

2 Introduction of characters, time, place, and situation

OUTLINE: TELLING YOUR EXPERIENCE FOR ENJOYMENT

RISING ACTION

1 Events of the story in chronological order

2 Climax (highest point; plan it carefully)

OUTLINE: TELLING YOUR EXPERIENCE FOR ENJOYMENT

CONCLUSION

CHECK LIST FOR EMOTIONAL EFFECT

1. Did I use much specific detail in descriptions?
2. Did I give causes and evidences of emotions?
3. Did I act out the characters?
4. Did I use dialogue wherever possible?

NOTES:

OUTLINE: TELLING YOUR EXPERIENCE FOR ENJOYMENT

EXPOSITION

1 Statement to arouse curiosity

2 Introduction of characters, time, place, and situation

OUTLINE: TELLING YOUR EXPERIENCE FOR ENJOYMENT

RISING ACTION

1 Events of the story in chronological order

2 Climax (highest point; plan it carefully)

OUTLINE: TELLING YOUR EXPERIENCE FOR ENJOYMENT

CONCLUSION

CHECK LIST FOR EMOTIONAL EFFECT

1. Did I use much specific detail in descriptions?
2. Did I give causes and evidences of emotions?
3. Did I act out the characters?
4. Did I use dialogue wherever possible?

NOTES:

INSTRUCTOR'S EVALUATION:

TELLING YOUR EXPERIENCE FOR ENJOYMENT

1 Material

  A. Exposition

	Excellent	Good	Fair	Poor
1. Arousing curiosity				
2. Describing characters				
3. Setting time				
4. Describing place				
5. Establishing conflict				

  B. Rising action

	Excellent	Good	Fair	Poor
1. Developing suspense				
2. Using setbacks				
3. Using dilemmas				
4. Building climax				

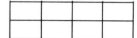

  C. Conclusion

	Excellent	Good	Fair
1. Including essential information			
2. Omitting unnecessary details			

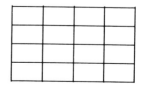

  D. Emotional effect

	Excellent	Good	Fair	Poor
1. Using specific detail in descriptions				
2. Giving causes and evidences of emotions				
3. Acting out characters				
4. Using dialogue				

INSTRUCTOR'S EVALUATION:
TELLING YOUR EXPERIENCE FOR ENJOYMENT

	Excellent	Good	Fair	Poor

2 Delivery

   A. Voice

   B. Enthusiasm

   C. Posture

   D. Appearance

   E. Gestures

   F. Eye contact

   G. Movement

3 Comments

GRADE _____   INSTRUCTOR _____

NOTE: The instructor's evaluation sheet that is provided in each chapter is to be given to your instructor with his or her copy of your outline, for use in evaluating your presentation.

3

TELLING YOUR
EXPERIENCE TO
MAKE A POINT

This assignment provides a transition between Parts 1 and 2, Communicating for Enjoyment and Communicating to Inform, because telling your experience to make a point involves both purposes. In the most enjoyable conversations, people often tell stories about their experiences primarily for enjoyment but at the same time to make a point about some topic under discussion. That is, the story is told in a certain context, and it has some significance beyond the merely personal.

When you want to make a point, the most persuasive way to back it up is often by describing your own experience. Properly told, a personal story can clarify your meaning and support your argument. It also communicates a good deal about you as a person: by showing that you have experience with the topic at hand, it presents your credentials as an authority of sorts. And if you want to, you can select, organize, and emphasize details in the story in such a way that they suggest many additional things about your personality, your ability, your efficiency—in other words, about your whole manner of thinking and working.

ASSIGNMENT

You are a product of your experience. You are largely what you believe you are, and what you believe you are has been developed by all the experiences—both successes and failures—in your life. Did you decide that people are unselfish because someone did you a good turn? Did you change your mind about becoming a pharmacist because you flunked

31

chemistry? Did you begin to feel you were unattractive because you didn't have a date for an important party during high school? Did an unfortunate experience with a used car salesman cause you to be wary of car salesmen?

Give some careful thought to the experiences that have molded your concepts of yourself and your environment. Select one that has clearly influenced your thoughts or actions and organize it for presentation to your class.

PRELIMINARY ORGANIZATION

As in the last assignment, limit yourself to a very specific experience so that you can tell it in detail, and use your memory and imagination to reconstruct the experience vividly and concretely. Pay special attention to details that will make clear the effect that the experience had on your attitude toward yourself and your environment. For your own benefit, reevaluate the experience—were your conclusions justified at the time, and do they still hold up today?

As before, you should organize your story in three parts: the exposition, the rising action and climax, and the conclusion. Be sure that the exposition contains a statement to arouse curiosity and presents a clear picture of the time, place, characters, and situation; that the rising action contains all the important events in chronological order and builds toward the climax; and that the conclusion includes only essential information.

When you use a story to make a point, you have three main techniques to choose from. One possibility is to leave the point unstated but to imply it very clearly through the details and events you include in the story and through the way you present them. This is the most difficult technique of the three, and its subtlety makes it more suitable for written than for oral communication. A reader can review a story to check his or her impressions, but a listener cannot.

A second technique is to state the point first and then tell the experience. This is called the deductive method, and it is frequently used in purely expository speaking and writing. In speaking that emphasizes a narrative, however, stating the point at the beginning may telegraph the ending and thus destroy the suspense that holds audience attention through the exposition and rising action.

The best organizational pattern for this assignment is probably the inductive pattern, in which you tell your story first and then state your point in the conclusion. You will have several opportunities to use a deductive organization in Part 2, Communicating to Inform, so this time try using the inductive pattern.

DEVELOPMENT

Follow the suggestions for development given in Chapter 2, Telling Your Experience for Enjoyment. Also review the composite list of strengths and weaknesses you made after the last assignment. Try in this assignment to make good use of your strengths and to improve your weak areas.

Be sure to include all important details that lead up to your point. In your exposition, make clear directly or by implication how you felt before your experience. During the rising action, include your transitional thoughts about the problems and dilemmas you faced, and about possible solutions. These will prepare for your conclusion, so that it will not seem too abrupt. In your conclusion, emphasize the outcomes—happy or unhappy—that solidified your thinking. In making your point at the end, state it very carefully and as specifically as possible. Do not over-generalize.

If your point seems entirely based on this one experience, you may be vulnerable to the charge of hasty generalization. If you ask yourself whether your generalization is really justified and can answer "yes," then some of your other experiences or observations probably also support your point. If they occurred before the experience you are telling, include them in your exposition, as part of your thoughts and character development. If they came during your experience, include them in the rising action; if they came afterward, include them in your conclusion.

At this point it would be helpful to analyze the sample manuscript at the end of this chapter. Then make two copies of your story outline on the forms provided. Give one outline to your instructor, with the blank evaluation form provided for his or her use, and keep the other outline for your own use in practicing and delivering your story.

PRACTICE

Rehearse your speech aloud until you have your material and delivery under control. Watch yourself in a mirror to keep your gestures and facial expressions natural. Listen to yourself for natural vocal inflections. Use exaggeration wherever appropriate.

DELIVERY

As before, adopt an alert posture; look at every member of your audience before and during your presentation; be natural, enthusiastic, energetic, and friendly. In addition, this time, work on your entrance and exit. They determine the first and last impressions that you make on your audience. When your turn comes, walk firmly and confidently to the front of the class, take your position, and pause. During this pause, look and smile at your whole audience in a friendly manner; then take a deep breath to begin your speech with. At the end of your presentation, deliver your last line with vocal punch, so that your listeners *know* it is the last line, and pause briefly before you walk firmly and confidently back to your seat. If you start to leave while you are saying your last line, it suggests to the audience that you are eager to get away from them. Besides implying that you either dislike your audience or lack confidence, a premature departure weakens your ending, which contains the whole point of your story.

CRITICISM

When you criticize the presentations of others, follow the suggestions given in the previous assignment. In addition, evaluate the point of each story. Is the point really a logical outcome of the experience? Is it properly limited? Has the speaker included the observations and considerations that led up to it? As before, make your criticisms positive and constructive. Tell the speaker what he or she did well and make suggestions for improvement. To assist you, use the listening forms for this assignment described in Chapter 13. Remember, don't allow yourself to be merely a fault-finder.

SAMPLE STUDENT MANUSCRIPT

(1)   Little did I know what I was getting myself into the day my sister talked me into buying a sun lamp. All I had to do was to pay for half. My sister, Carol, explained that for just two or three dollars I could enjoy the advantages of a beautiful, sexy sun tan all year round. I must admit that the idea sounded like a good investment. I agreed to buy half the lamp.

(2)   Five minutes later I found myself speeding down the highway en route to a nearby electric store. When we arrived, we carefully inspected their selection of lamps, which consisted of one General Electric model that was priced at twelve dollars! After discovering the price, I was ready to forget the whole idea, but Carol argued that another couple of dollars for a year's worth of a beautiful tan was worth it.

(3)   When we brought the lamp home, you could guess who was first to try it out, my sister. She spent at least half an hour hogging the lamp, allowing me only to stick an occasional hand under as long as I didn't cast a shadow on her.

(4)   After a few days, I was fortunate enough to use the lamp for myself. I read the directions carefully. It said to use for six minutes at a time and that the lamp was good for about a thousand applications. I turned it on and sat there for six minutes, allowing the rays to penetrate while dreaming about the beautiful tan I would have the next day.

(5)   The next morning I sprang out of bed and ran to the nearest mirror. To my utter surprise I was just as pale—if not more so—as the day before. That night I decided to use at least a double or triple application. As I lay under the lamp, my eyes felt irritated. I discovered the next morning they were very bloodshot, but I had a little bit of a sun tan. I expected at school that everyone would notice my tan. All anyone said, however, was, "You must have been up late last night. Your eyes are all bloodshot."

(6)   Later I discovered, through some of my friends, that a sun lamp could be used to lighten or bleach one's hair somewhat. Because I always wanted my hair to be lighter, I decided to try it. After many days of hard tedious work, I received nothing but a sunburned scalp. Needless to say, my hair-color remained the same.

(7)   Thinking with a logical mind, I counted the number of times I used the lamp. I did this to compute the number of applications that were left out of the original one thousand. I expected my sister had done the same, but, when I was on about seventeenth application, I discovered that Carol had lent our lamp to her friends—and everybody's relatives—numerous times. I was beginning to think she was seeking revenge for some terrible deed I had done to her in the past.

(8)   The worst experience with the lamp of all, however, was when I wanted to have a sun tan before a very important date. This was a special date that I had planned for three weeks. It was my date's birthday. We were to go to dinner and then to a live show. To make matters worse, it

was my first date with her. Because of all this I wanted to look my best. The night before, I decided to use the sun lamp. I allowed ten minutes on one side of my face and then rolled over to expose the other side. Suddenly I grew very sleepy. When I looked at my watch again I found that an hour and ten minutes had passed. What could I do now . . . burn the other side?

(9) That morning I unwillingly stared at the mirror only to see a half-normal face, and half-sunburned, red face. I explained to my date that I fell asleep at the beach and have learned from that point on to stay away from artificial things and be as natural as possible.

QUESTIONS FOR DISCUSSION

1. How much of this story is exposition?

2. The exposition does not set the time or place. Are they needed?

3. What makes the opening sentence effective?

4. What clues do you find to the character of the sister?

5. What inner thoughts does the author express?

6. Are there any dilemmas? any setbacks?

7. Where is the climax? How could the development of the climax be improved?

8. How much of the story is conclusion?

9. Is the point stated in the last sentence properly limited and logical in terms of the experience related?

OUTLINE: TELLING YOUR EXPERIENCE TO MAKE A POINT

EXPOSITION

1 Statement to arouse curiosity

2 Introduction of characters, time, place, and situation

OUTLINE: TELLING YOUR EXPERIENCE TO MAKE A POINT

RISING ACTION

1 Events of the story in chronological order

2 Climax (highest point; plan it carefully)

OUTLINE: TELLING YOUR EXPERIENCE TO MAKE A POINT

CONCLUSION

1 Resolution of story

2 Point

OUTLINE: TELLING YOUR EXPERIENCE TO MAKE A POINT

CHECK LIST FOR POINT

1. Is the point a logical outcome of my experience?
2. Is the point properly limited?
3. Have I included the observations and considerations that led up to my point?

OUTLINE: TELLING YOUR EXPERIENCE TO MAKE A POINT

EXPOSITION

1 Statement to arouse curiosity

2 Introduction of characters, time, place, and situation

OUTLINE: TELLING YOUR EXPERIENCE TO MAKE A POINT

RISING ACTION

1 Events of the story in chronological order

2 Climax (highest point; plan it carefully)

OUTLINE: TELLING YOUR EXPERIENCE TO MAKE A POINT

CONCLUSION

1 Resolution of story

2 Point

OUTLINE: TELLING YOUR EXPERIENCE TO MAKE A POINT

CHECK LIST FOR POINT

1. Is the point a logical outcome of my experience?
2. Is the point properly limited?
3. Have I included the observations and considerations that led up to my point?

INSTRUCTOR'S EVALUATION:
TELLING YOUR EXPERIENCE TO MAKE A POINT

1 Material

   A. Exposition

      1. Arousing curiosity

      2. Describing characters

      3. Setting time

      4. Describing place

   B. Rising action

      1. Developing suspense

      2. Using setbacks

      3. Using dilemmas

      4. Building climax

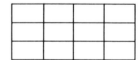

   C. Conclusion

      1. Including essential information

      2. Omitting unnecessary details

      3. Statement of point

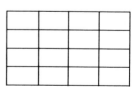

   D. Emotional effect

      1. Using specific detail in descriptions

      2. Giving causes and evidences of emotions

      3. Acting out characters

      4. Using dialogue

The rating columns for each section are: Excellent, Good, Fair, Poor.

INSTRUCTOR'S EVALUATION:
TELLING YOUR EXPERIENCE TO MAKE A POINT

	Excellent	Good	Fair	Poor
E. Development of point				
1. Giving thoughts and observations that led up to it				
2. Showing that point is a logical outcome of the experience				

2 Delivery

	Excellent	Good	Fair	Poor
A. Voice				
B. Enthusiasm				
C. Posture				
D. Appearance				
E. Gestures				
F. Eye contact				
G. Movement				
H. Entrance				
I. Exit				

3 Comments

GRADE _____   INSTRUCTOR _____

2
COMMUNICATING TO INFORM

People are interested in you, and they are also interested in what you know. If you make an effort to share your knowledge with your friends, you may be surprised to find out how much you have to say that they will enjoy hearing about, and—perhaps even more important—how much of value they will share with you in return.

Don't make the mistake of assuming that you don't know anything worth telling about. Each person's experience is unique, and you haven't lived all these years without learning a great many things that will be new and interesting to those around you. If you do not share what you know with others, they will not assume that you know nothing; they will assume that you don't consider them worthy of your attention. When I was in college, I found out to my surprise that some of my friends thought I was conceited. When I asked one of them why, she said it was because I never stopped to talk. I always seemed too busy. This was ironic, because I really did want to stop and talk. Perhaps out of shyness, I assumed I had nothing to say that anyone would want to hear, so I tried to look busy just to protect my pride. After that I made a point of stopping to talk. My friends and I learned a lot from each other—including how to be better friends.

Your communication experiences in this section will call upon you to examine your knowledge and to find meaningful ways to communicate it to others. If something interests you, you can make it interest them. Show them, specifically and with enthusiasm, **why** it interests you. When you prepare each speech, evaluate your knowledge. If you find it lacking, do some research, some interviewing, or some observing. Get the specific facts that support your ideas. But in addition, **be sure to communicate yourself.** If you do, your listeners' interest in you will sharpen their interest in the subject.

Speaking to inform (expository speaking) involves teaching something. You must gather the facts concerning your topic and explain them to your listeners. You may explain how to do something, what something is, how it works, how it is used, how it developed, and so forth. Communicating to inform will add to your own knowledge about things that interest you, increase your ability to share that knowledge, and allow you to give others, at no cost to yourself, something that they will truly value.

UNEMPLOYMENT: THE FOUR STAGES

MONICA E. BREIDENBACH

The author of this article, Monica E. Breidenbach, is director of research and development with Pierson Associates, a career consulting firm based in Washington, D.C. The material is similar in purpose, organization, and development to the assignments in Part 2. Give it a first reading now. Later on, you will be asked to reread it and to analyze it, using the discussion questions that follow the article, in order to help you understand the assignments in Part 2 and improve your own communication.

Is the daily grind just that—a grind? Is job satisfaction something you dream about? Do you have difficulty getting up in the morning? All these are telltale signs that your job is at a standstill. When you face up to it, you might decide to tell the boss you quit. Or, before you have the chance, your disillusionment could lead to your being fired. In either case, once you find yourself—as we all do sooner or later—in the ranks of the unemployed and searching for a new career, look out! The unemployment experience can put you on "cloud nine" one week, and cause you to sink to the depths of depression the next.

You won't be alone. Most unemployed people seem to experience four distinct mood stages as they try to adjust to being out of a job. How long you remain in each state of mind and motivation is a personal decision. A stage may last one day, or it may stretch out for weeks, months—even years.

It makes little difference if you've been fired, resigned inopportunely or deliberately decided to move on to a new job or career: the four stages occur in each case, and they must be recognized to be handled effectively. Glossing over or denying them will only compound the problem. On the other hand, facing them, naming them, and when necessary, choosing appropriate alternate behavior patterns are the steps needed to

"Unemployment: The Four Stages" by Monica E. Breidenbach. From Women's Work magazine, vol. 4, no. 3, May/June 1978. Reprinted with permission of Women's Work, Inc., 1302 18th St. N.W., Suite 203, Washington, D. C.

49

project yourself beyond the "four stages" and into a new career position.

The initial reaction to being unemployed is inevitably optimism: "I'll get another job easily!" "XYZ Corporation would love to have someone with my skills." "I'm a well-educated individual with years of experience in the work world." "I'll be on another payroll very shortly." Or, depending on the degree of previous job frustration: "Hurrah. The monkey's off my back." "Now I'm free to explore other possibilities." "Let's take a short vacation before I go back to looking for another job: we owe it to ourselves to celebrate being rid of this awful situation once and for all."

Such an attitude may be unrealistic . . . but it's not unlikely. That's because frequently the frustrated human spirit responds to sudden release with a great surge of optimism, not unlike an incorrectly opened champagne bottle. You're overflowing with bubbly pronouncements of a rosy future that's yours for the asking. While it is undeniably crucial to keep up your attitude and self-confidence during the entire unemployment experience, exaggerated optimism can lead to behavior that won't further your goal to become employed once more. You're only cheating yourself if you use positive mental attitude statements to bolster your bruised ego to the extent that you become unrealistic about your situation.

Sliding down from optimism you can quickly hit the inertia stage. At this point, suddenly the most aggressive and competent people find themselves grasping at any straw of an excuse to postpone taking positive action toward finding a job: "I guess I've hit a slump." "I don't feel like doing all that work right now." "It's no use; I've been out of the job market too long." "I need the extra rest." "I deserve a long vacation after working so hard for nothing all those years." "There'll be time for looking for a job later when the season is better. No one hires when the weather is bad."

When inertia strikes, ordinarily industrious people become temporarily immobilized; motivating themselves to focus on a career search, to identify resources and to channel their energies into the search seems to be more than they can master.

Allowed to develop unchecked, these progressive states can result in *depression*. The depression stage of unemployment is readily identifiable, but difficult to escape. Depression takes many forms: sleeping more, frequent illnesses, lethargy, wanting to be alone, feeling sorry for one's self, discouragement, frustration . . . the list is endless. Depression can also lead to physical illness. This depressed state of health further antagonizes the spirit of unemployed persons and reinforces negative concepts about their ability to achieve.

Dark and lonely as it is at the bottom, the depression stage usually holds the seeds of the final and most constructive of the four unemployment phases: the *confrontation* stage. At some point, you begin to come face to face with the truth: that, until now, through the ups and downs of the preceding three stages, you have not been looking at your job and career situation realistically. This is the time for the hard questions—and the even harder answers.

What do I want? What is required to get there? What do I have to offer right now? What do I need to put myself in a competitive situation to meet my career goals? Am I prepared to spend the time, money, energy, etc., to prepare myself?

Even if your dreams require a career change, it is possible that they can be realized as long as you take a conscious look at all the ramifications. Identify the effect such a change could have on your life. You cannot be a pianist at 40, for example, if you don't have the talent or the training. Looking at dream careers realistically isn't easy for any career changer. Some dreams need to be put aside once and for all; but many can be realized.

And, remember, it's not just the beginning careerists who question their choices; even the most recognized and successful professionals often reach a time in life when they begin to experience less and less job or career satisfaction. Life experience, other people's influence, personal tragedy, achievements, and job stagnation all contribute to this feeling.

This phenomenon has many names in today's pop psychology; the most common is "mid-life crisis," which finds a parallel in "mid-career change." Here, your attitude is the key to getting control, since these two "crisis points" can be viewed either as a challenge or as a reason for sinking back into the depression stage.

Whether you're a relative newcomer in the job market, a top-notch professional or a mid-life crisis sufferer, you're likely to feel a bit threatened by the notion of beginning again. Your desire for change will help overcome some of the fears that abound whenever moving from security to new beginnings. Examine each of your unrealistic fears, such as, "I'm too old," "I don't have the correct or enough education," "I have no experience in the area," "No one will want to listen to my ideas."

Above all, be realistic about your strengths as well as your weaknesses. Remember, a realistic "re-awakening" will lead you out of the depression stage and into the fruitful *confrontation* phase of your unemployment.

At this time, as you begin to assess your situation, take a look at the history you have created, and determine what you want your future to be like. It's not easy. Sometimes, realizing you are responsible for where you are is a disagreeable pill to swallow. Deciding what the next step in your job or career search will be is the challenge. Remember: it's up to you to take control of directing your future.

As you move into an honest self-assessment, or *confrontation*, you are embarking on an exercise which not only can enhance your job and career potential, but may also lead you to learn new things about yourself and help you discover aspects of your skills and possibilities which you had never thought of before. To complete a successful confrontation stage, you should be prepared to:

1) identify your career goals;
2) set priorities;
3) align career goals with your life goals;
4) explore the potential options;
5) assess the total problem;
6) evaluate the best time to make your move; and
7) strategize the most effective campaign to insure moving into a new job or career successfully.

Your chief motivation force at this stage should be knowing that you are the architect of your future. This does not mean you won't still experience days of inertia or depression now and then. But, by constantly confronting yourself with your career potential and life goals, you won't remain in these states for long.

As you pursue your career, keep in mind that focusing your energies and resources to highlight different skills at different times gives variety to your "career life." When career change becomes necessary, you then have many building blocks ready to rearrange for a dynamic new career. Select the appropriate time to change your job or career. Also, you must consider the overall consequences of such a move: How will it affect your lifestyle? Will there be much travel? Will you have to relocate? Will you have new responsibilities?

Customizing and strategizing an effective job or career search involves research, discipline, interviewing, network building and resume writing. But the most effective aspect is a positive self-image. Knowing whether inertia, depression or frustration is dominating your life at any given time is not enough. These identifiable stages one goes through in job and career transition are signs that your professional life is out of control. And control is the key to managing a personal career path effectively. It means maximizing your resources to attain pre-determined goals that will develop into a satisfying career pattern.

QUESTIONS FOR DISCUSSION

1. What is the thesis, and what are the main points?

2. Is there a summary? Is one needed?

3. How is each main point developed?

4. Is testimony used anywhere in the article? Is it needed?

5. The author does not refer to her own experience. Where and how might it be effective to do so?

6. Each main point in this article is given very minimal development. If you wished to expand the development of the main points, what kind of material would you add? What considerations of purpose and audience would govern your selection of additional material?

7. Many people object to words like "customizing," "strategizing," and "maximizing." What are your feelings about the effectiveness of this kind of language?

8. The author has simplified and clarified her knowledge about unemployment by classification. Can you similarly classify your own knowledge about how to do something?

9. If you wanted to develop this topic with visual aids (see Chapter 5) or anecdotes (Chapter 6), how would you do it?

4
GIVING A DEMONSTRATION

Communicating is partly a physical process. Your words and tone of voice account for only about half of the total impact you make on your listeners.* The rest is communicated physically, through facial expression, posture, gesture, and so forth. Nervousness, for example, is communicated by shaking knees, or a worried frown, or a series of small, indefinite, uncompleted movements.

You communicate most effectively when you "say" the same thing physically that you say vocally. If the two are different, your listeners will probably pay more attention to what you do than to what you say. The maxim "Don't believe anything you hear and only about half of what you see" suggests that your listeners would be right. What you do may indeed be more revealing, and more reliable, than what you say. If a person's knees, hands, and voice shook as he told you that he wasn't nervous, what would you think?

Physical action can, of course, suggest many positive things about you: knowledge, vitality, conviction, enthusiasm, and an eagerness to communicate. It can suggest an interesting, vital person who knows how to get things done and has the energy to carry plans through.

Giving a demonstration will require you to make planned, meaningful movements part of your speaking style. Besides practicing physical communication when you give your own demonstration, notice when others speak how many things they communicate through facial expression, posture, and gesture. For your own benefit, make a mental note of techniques you can borrow to use yourself.

---

*A UCLA psychologist has a formula for this: Total Impact = .07 verbal + .38 vocal + .55 facial. (Albert Mehrabian, "Communication Without Words," *Psychology Today*, September 1968.)

Think about the skills you have—the things you know how to do. Select one that you do well or enjoy a great deal, preferably one that requires the use of your hands, arms, legs, or body, and plan to explain and demonstrate it to your listeners.

SUBJECT

Golf, baseball, football, artificial respiration, first aid, fly casting, shooting a gun, exercising, dancing, walking, or sitting—any one of these, or something similar, would be a suitable subject for your speech.

TOPIC

Narrow the subject down to a specific topic. For example, "The Four-step Approach in Delivering a Bowling Ball" makes a better topic than "How to Bowl." (It would take at least twenty minutes just to explain the scoring.) Here are some other specific topics: How to putt, how to pitch a curve, how to pass a football, how to revive a drowning person, how to put a splint on a broken arm, how to do the latest dance, how to do the basic ballet positions, how to play the guitar, how to sit down gracefully, how to make a French omelette, how to do some basic isometric exercises, how to remove the cork from a wine bottle, how to breathe correctly, how to lift weights, how to cast a fishing rod, how to return a tennis ball, how to apply a tourniquet, how to shoot a basketball.

THESIS

Write a simple declarative sentence announcing your topic. You should do this now, even though it will not be the first sentence in your talk, so that you can refer to the statement as you plan the rest of the speech. It is probably best to use an "I'm going to tell you" kind of sentence, so that your audience will recognize it as the announcement of your purpose. Here are some examples: "I would like to show you how to return a tennis ball"; "I will demonstrate the proper way to apply a tourniquet"; "I intend to show you four different types of basketball shots."

MAIN POINTS

Now plan the main points and the organizational pattern of your speech. For a talk on how to return a tennis ball, you might use a topical pattern: (1) the grip, (2) the stance, (3) the swing. For a talk on how to apply a tourniquet, you might use a time-order pattern: (1) wrap the material tightly around the limb and tie a half-knot, (2) place a short stick on the half-knot and tie a full knot, (3) twist the stick to tighten the tourniquet until the flow of blood stops, (4) hold the stick in place with the loose ends of the tourniquet, (5) take the patient to a doctor. For a talk on four types of basketball shots you might use classification: (1) set shot, (2) hook shot, (3) jump shot, (4) lay-up. Regardless of which organizational pattern you use, your main points should be parallel in construction (worded the same) for emphasis and coherence.

As you introduce each main point in your speech, repeat the key words from your thesis. "The first step in applying a tourniquet is to . . . ," "The second step in applying a tourniquet is to . . . ," and so forth. This will remind the audience of your topic and show how each main point relates to your purpose and to the other main points.

DEVELOPMENT

Develop the body of your speech before planning the introduction and conclusion in detail. First, define unfamiliar or vague words and develop each main point fully. Explain why it is important to perform the activity in the way you demonstrate. There are several ways to make that clear. You can point out what will happen if it's done wrong; you can use examples, drawn from your experiences or ones you've witnessed, that emphasize the importance of your method; you can employ an appeal to authority by quoting an expert—a doctor if your topic is tourniquets, a winner of the Davis Cup if your topic is tennis, and so forth.

Now plan the introduction and the conclusion. It is important that you plan them after you have developed the body of the speech to be sure that they focus attention on the body and do not use up important ideas or developmental materials that belong in the body. The introduction, which comes first in the actual speech, should lead to the body, and the conclusion, which comes last, should refer back to it. Although they are relatively short (combined, they should not take more than one-third of your total time), they represent your first and last impressions on your audience. So plan them carefully.

In planning the introduction, first get the audience's attention. You might try (1) a startling statement or question, (2) a story about an experience (yours or someone else's) related to your topic, (3) a short explanation of why you chose this topic for this audience, or (4) statistics or a quotation that emphasizes the importance of your topic. Secondly, indicate to your audience why you think they ought to know what you're going to show them (refer to the section on audience analysis in Chapter 14 and be very specific about the interests of *this* audience). For most of the sample topics given here, the most likely reasons are *participant interest* and *spectator interest.* That is, either the audience will want you to show them how to do it so that they can do it themselves (participant interest), or they will want you to show them how to do it so that they will enjoy it more when they see someone else do it (spectator interest). Since your presentation of some topics will depend on which interest you are developing, you may have to choose between the two and make the choice clear to your audience. At the end of your introduction, announce the topic in your thesis.

In planning the conclusion, first summarize what you have said by repeating the topic and the main points. After that, you may assume that your listeners have the material clearly in mind. Close your speech by telling them what to do with it. Would you suggest that they begin practicing, attending events, taking a class, reading more on the subject? Do you think they should simply remember it for some future occasion that might arise? If you point out some immediate or future use for the material, they may make a point of remembering it. If you don't, they may make a point of forgetting it. Your closing appeal should in some way refer back to the interest you developed in the introduction. Be sure your closing shows a high degree of friendliness and concern for your audience.

At this point, you should reread and analyze "Unemployment: The Four Stages," which begins on page 49, and the sample outline at the end of this chapter. Compare the organization and development of these with your own. Then make two copies of the detailed outline for your speech, on the forms provided. Give one outline to your instructor, with the blank evaluation form provided for his or her use, and keep the other outline for your own use.

PRACTICE

Working from your detailed outline, rehearse your speech aloud. Practice both the wording and the actions for timing. Plan your posture and appearance to make a positive impression on your audience. Think about where you will place yourself and your audience so that they will be able to see the demonstration. If you show each movement from different angles and at different speeds, you can be sure everyone is able to see, and repetition will also help them remember what you've demonstrated.

Practice part of the time in front of a mirror and part of the time with your family or friends. When you feel that you know what you want to say and how you want to say it, make a brief key-word outline for use in the actual delivery of the speech. Continue practicing with the key-word outline until you feel that you have absolute control over yourself and your material.

DELIVERY

When your turn comes, walk firmly and confidently to the front of the class. Face your audience squarely, with your body erect and alert and with your weight evenly distributed on both feet. Before you begin talking, look around the room at every member of your audience. Show them by the expression on your face and by your manner that you are pleased they are there and that you welcome the opportunity to address them. Then take a good, deep breath and begin in a strong, clear voice. If you sound confident, you will get courage from the sound and actually become confident. If you begin in a weak, shaky voice, your audience will lose confidence in you, and you may too.

During your speech keep your voice strong and firm. Pronounce all words clearly and distinctly. Emphasize important points (especially your statement of purpose and your main points) by saying them louder or slower than usual or by pausing before and after them.

Vigorous gestures and movements will hold audience attention and use up nervous energy; you will be both more effective and more comfortable if you use them. When you make a gesture, be sure you complete it. If you drop a gesture in the middle it is left hanging in the air, where it weakens your presentation by interfering with the next idea.

Each movement should have a purpose, of course. You go to the blackboard to write; you move away from the speaker's stand to make your demonstration visible to your audience; and so forth. Be sure the purpose is clear to your audience. When you make a move, decide where you want to go, go there, and stop. Don't let your movements become indefinite and weak.

Keep your voice firm and clear all the way to the end of the speech. Give your final line vocal punch; don't let it fade out gradually. Stay in position at the front of the room as you deliver your last sentence, and stand still for a moment afterwards to give the audience time to absorb its impact. Then turn and walk confidently back to your seat.

During the speech, maintain good eye contact. Keep your manner friendly, direct, confident, and enthusiastic. You can be sure that your audience will enjoy your speech if you show them by your manner that you enjoy talking to them.

CRITICISM

When you are called upon to criticize the speeches of others, either orally or in writing, be positive and constructive. First point out specifically what was effective about the speech, so that the speaker can maintain and develop his or her strong points. Then point out specifically how the speech could be improved. This does not necessarily mean something was wrong; it simply means that the speech was less than perfect. In most cases you will probably think that the speaker had a good idea but could have improved the way he or she developed or presented it. However good a speech may be, you have a responsibility to make suggestions so that the speaker can continue to improve. Be sure to participate in discussions about the speeches of your classmates, whether you agree or disagree with the points others make. The speaker has a right to know how the whole audience felt about his or her presentation.

When receiving comments on your own speeches, don't be too quick to defend what you have done—or too quick to decide you were wrong. Accept helpful suggestions gracefully, apply the ones you think will work, and disregard those that will not. You should use your classmates' comments as a source of ideas, as a way to be sure you have seen and considered all the alternatives and have selected the best material and delivery pattern for you, your topic, and your audience. But you are the final authority on what's right for you.

SAMPLE STUDENT OUTLINE

INTRODUCTION

I According to the *Palo Alto Times* of September 13, Victor Alessandro, musical director of the San Antonio Symphony, stabbed himself in the hand with his baton while rehearsing the orchestra.

A. The wound had to be closed with several stitches.

B. This illustrates just how "physical" conducting an orchestra can become.

II I would like to show you a bit of what goes into conducting not an orchestra but a choir.

A. The gestures used for both are essentially the same.

B. My own experiences have been with choir conducting.

C. I don't use a baton, so for me it has not been quite as hazardous an undertaking as it was for poor Mr. Alessandro.

III If you were suddenly in charge of directing a choir, as I once was, one of the most important things to teach the group would be how to follow the conductor.

BODY

I Conductors use more or less standard gestures to indicate the various meters. The first beat in all meters is marked by a decisive downbeat directly in front of the conductor's body, but from that point on the patterns vary according to the meter.

A. The simplest of all rhythms is a 2/4, or simple duple meter.

1. The standard gesture for this beat is a down, up.

2. A march such as "The American Patrol" would be a good example.

B. A 3/4, or simple triple meter, is next in difficulty.

1. This is conducted like a triangle.

2. An example of a triple meter is a waltz such as the "Merry Widow Waltz."

C. Next in difficulty would be the 4/4, or common time, beat.

1. Leon Dallin, author of *Foundation in Music Theory*, says,

61

"A 'C' in a time signature, a vestige of an older system, is used interchangeably with 4/4."

2. 4/4 time is conducted thus: (demonstrate).

3. "Hark the Herald Angels Sing" is a good example of a 4/4 beat.

D. A 6/8 rhythm can be conducted in two ways.

1. The slow 6/8, as in "Drink to Me Only with Thine Eyes," is conducted thus: (demonstrate).

2. A fast 6/8 is conducted just the same as a 2/4.

a. An example of this beat is "For He's a Jolly Good Fellow."

b. If this were conducted the slow way, the conductor would look like a wound-up toy.

II Conductors also use gestures to show other things besides the actual beats in a song.

A. He or she shows volume change.

1. When the conductor wants a louder sound, he or she uses large gestures.

2. A smaller sound is shown by using small gestures.

B. In a choir the conductor must use a gesture to get the choir to stand up all together.

C. He or she must also indicate by gesture when to sit down.

D. The conductor must also gesture a cut-off or finish of a song.

CONCLUSION

I The gestures I have shown you are but a few of the many basic movements used in conducting.

II Great conductors such as Leonard Bernstein, Josef Krips, and others embellish a good deal on these patterns. Next time you watch the Schola Cantorum perform, keep your eyes on Mr. Stanton. Perhaps you will find it challenging, as I do, to try to interpret all his very active movements.

BIBLIOGRAPHY

Leon Dallin, *Foundations in Music Theory*. Belmont, California: Wadsworth Publishing Company, Inc., 1962.

Palo Alto Times, September 13, 1967.

QUESTIONS FOR DISCUSSION

1. What is the thesis? Is it a good one?

2. What are the main points? Are they well worded?

3. What is the purpose of Introduction I?

4. What is the purpose of Introduction II?

5. Is there a summary? Is one needed?

6. What is the purpose of Conclusion II?

7. How do I A, B, C, D in the body of the speech relate to each other?

8. How do II A, B, C, D in the body of the speech relate to each other?

9. Is this a suitable topic for the assignment?

10. Which points in the body of the speech would require demonstration?

11. Why are examples like "The American Patrol" and "Hark the Herald Angels Sing" used?

12. What basic audience interest in the topic is developed? How do you know?

OUTLINE: GIVING A DEMONSTRATION

Subject:

Topic:

INTRODUCTION

1 Attention device

2 Need

3 Thesis (statement of purpose)

OUTLINE: GIVING A DEMONSTRATION

BODY

Main points (not less than two or more than five; parallel in wording; clearly related to each other and to your purpose) and support for each point

OUTLINE: GIVING A DEMONSTRATION

CONCLUSION

1 Summary

2 Closing appeal

OUTLINE: GIVING A DEMONSTRATION

3 Bibliography (if needed)

CHECK LIST FOR PHYSICAL ACTIONS

1. Am I standing with my weight on both feet in an alert, erect posture?
2. Am I really looking at my audience throughout the speech?
3. Am I using planned, meaningful gestures and movements?
4. Am I carrying out my movements and gestures with strength and purpose?
5. Is my demonstration clearly visible to my audience?
6. Have I shown movements at different angles and at different speeds wherever needed?

OUTLINE: GIVING A DEMONSTRATION

Subject:

Topic:

INTRODUCTION

1 Attention device

2 Need

3 Thesis (statement of purpose)

OUTLINE: GIVING A DEMONSTRATION

BODY

Main points (not less than two or more than five; parallel in wording; clearly related to each other and to your purpose) and support for each point

OUTLINE: GIVING A DEMONSTRATION

CONCLUSION

1 Summary

2 Closing appeal

OUTLINE: GIVING A DEMONSTRATION

3 Bibliography (if needed)

CHECK LIST FOR PHYSICAL ACTIONS

1. Am I standing with my weight on both feet in an alert, erect posture?
2. Am I really looking at my audience throughout the speech?
3. Am I using planned, meaningful gestures and movements?
4. Am I carrying out my movements and gestures with strength and purpose?
5. Is my demonstration clearly visible to my audience?
6. Have I shown movements at different angles and at different speeds wherever needed?

INSTRUCTOR'S EVALUATION:
GIVING A DEMONSTRATION

	Excellent	Good	Fair	Poor

1 Delivery

   A. Voice

   B. Enthusiasm

   C. Posture

   D. Appearance

   E. Gestures

   F. Eye contact

   G. Movement

2 Material

   A. Introduction

      1. Attention step

      2. Need step

      3. Thesis

   B. Body

      1. Main points

      2. Development

   C. Conclusion

      1. Summary

      2. Closing appeal

   D. Transitions

INSTRUCTOR'S EVALUATION:
GIVING A DEMONSTRATION

	Excellent	Good	Fair	Poor

3 Language
   A. Vocabulary
   B. Sentence structure

	Excellent	Good	Fair	Poor

4 Demonstration
   A. Timing of word and action
   B. Visibility

5 Comments

GRADE _____   INSTRUCTOR _____

5
USING VISUAL AIDS

Psychologists say that what people see has greater impact on them than what they hear; hence the old adage "Don't tell; show!" So, whenever possible, use visual aids to help you communicate. Among the important advantages they offer are these:

1. Clarity. Words are tricky. They don't always mean the same thing to your audience that they do to you. If your listeners can see what you're talking about as well as hear about it, they will understand more fully.

2. Audience attention. You'll find your audience much more attentive when you use visual aids. The longer the presentation, the more important visual aids become for maintaining attention.

3. Memory. Because your audience pays better attention and understands better, they will remember more of your material for a longer period of time. Besides that—and not to be overlooked in practical planning—visual aids help you remember what you plan to say.

4. Poise. Having visual aids to handle and point to gives you something to do with your hands and makes you feel more comfortable. It also involves you physically in your speech and encourages movement, which will strengthen the impression you make on your audience.

ASSIGNMENT

From the subjects that you know well, think about some that you find difficult to describe in words alone. Select one which you know well—perhaps an object, an activity, a process you learned about in a college course, a job, or a hobby that you especially enjoy. Prepare to give a talk, using visual aids, on this subject.

SUBJECT

Don't begin by asking yourself what visual aids you have to plan a speech about. Select a subject first; then ask yourself how you can use visual aids to present it. If you wish to explain a piece of equipment, you can show the equipment itself, pictures of it, or diagrams of its parts and operation. If you plan to explain a process or a procedure, you can use a chart or the blackboard to diagram it. If you wish to explain the layout of a physical plant, the structure of an object, or the location of a place, you can use diagrams, photographs, drawings, or maps.

TOPIC

Narrow your subject down to a specific topic, something you can cover in detail. Keep in mind that your purpose is to inform the audience, so what you tell them must be new to them in some way, and it must be something they can recognize as useful either now or in the future.

Here are some suitable topics, with suggestions on visual aids that might be used to present them:

The structure of a tooth (diagram or model)

How the eye works (diagram or model);
optical illusions (charts and pictures)

Grooming an animal (equipment and animal)

Process of distilling (diagram and equipment)

Strokes of a piston (diagram or cutaway model)

Ignition system of a car (diagram)

How an IBM card is coded (card and diagram)

How to arrange flowers (diagrams, pictures, and flowers)

How to draw in perspective (diagrams and pictures)

How to make pottery (equipment and pottery)

How to take blood pressure (equipment and
physical demonstration)

Safety equipment for skiers (equipment)

Kinds of surfboards (surfboards or diagrams)

Trends in fashions (pictures)

A proper diet (charts)

Areas of the stage (diagrams)

How to make some article of clothing (pattern, equipment, and physical demonstration)

These are only a few possibilities; use one of them if you like, or choose another if you prefer.

THESIS

Write a simple sentence, clearly stating your topic. As before, refer to yourself and to the audience to show that this is the announcement of your purpose: "I would like to show you how to groom a horse for showing"; "I will explain to you the process of distilling"; "Let us consider the safety equipment needed in skiing"; "I would like to show you the various kinds of surfboards."

MAIN POINTS

Now plan the main points you will cover in the body of your speech. Several types of organization are possible. If you explain the structure of a physical object, your main points will probably be parts of that object given in some spatial order, such as top to bottom, nearest to farthest, right to left, outside to inside. If you explain a process, each main point should be a step in the process, and the steps should be arranged in chronological order. If you describe the different forms that a thing can take (a surfboard, for example), each main point will be one form (one kind of surfboard). The different types should be arranged in order of familiarity, or importance, or difficulty (most to least, or least to most)—whichever will be clearest and most interesting for your audience. Be sure, once again, that you word your main points the same way and that you repeat the key words from your thesis, to emphasize your points and give coherence to your speech.

DEVELOPMENT

Define words that will be unfamiliar to the audience, and explain with specific facts the who, what, when, where, and how of each main point. If you confess the problems you had and the mistakes you made, when you first tried to learn about the topic, it will help you maintain a close relationship with your audience. They will like your modesty and sense of humor, and appreciate your effort to anticipate questions and problems they may have.

Use your imagination to select and make striking visual aids, and use your skill as a speaker to explain them. People can interpret pictures very subjectively, so explain your visual aids clearly to be sure that your listeners will see what you want them to see. Use stories from your own experience now and then, to indicate your knowledge, to communicate yourself as well as your ideas, and to maintain audience attention. Whenever appropriate, quote an expert on the topic (a teacher, a scientist, a writer) to give additional authority to your material and to show that you have carefully researched the subject.

Before you do research, exhaust your own store of information. Then examine it critically to see where you need additional facts and support. Research includes observing and interviewing as well as reading books and articles. Consider all possible sources, and gather more information from them than you can use so that you can select the material that will suit your purpose best and have the most meaning for your audience.

After your main points are fully and clearly developed, plan the introduction. Take a positive attitude: assume that other people will be interested in your topic. Then ask yourself why. What is there about this topic that appeals to you, and therefore will appeal to the people you know? Does it perhaps have something to offer them intellectually, physically, or financially? Whatever need the topic will serve, be sure to communicate it specifically to your audience before you announce your thesis.

Follow the suggestions given in the last assignment for steps in the introduction, and check the body of the speech to see that whatever audience interest you develop in the introduction is further developed under your main points.

Plan the conclusion last. It should summarize what you set out to do and what you have done. As you summarize, you may want to refer to your visual aids again.

After the summary, make an appeal for some sort of action. The information you have given the audience is useful; show them what they can do with it. That way they will make a point of remembering it instead of letting it go in one ear and out the other. The appeal for action should be related to what you said in the introduction about why your topic would interest the audience. This gives the speech unity, and also a definite end. It will appeal to the audience because it shows that your material has been focused on them from beginning to end.

At this point you should read and analyze the sample outline at the end of this chapter. See if you can develop similar strengths and avoid similar weaknesses in your own outline. Then make two copies of your detailed outline for your speech, on the forms provided. Give one outline to your instructor, with the blank evaluation form provided for his or her use, and keep the other outline for your own use in practicing and delivering the speech.

VISUAL AIDS

If you are using pictures, diagrams, equipment, or other visual aids that you are collecting or preparing in advance, make them large enough to be seen by everyone at once. Passing things around distracts an audience from a speech. It also interferes with the communication process, because it is important for everyone to get the verbal explanation and the visual image simultaneously. If you are drawing your own pictures, charts, and so forth, make them attractive and neat. Sloppy visual aids are hard to understand and make a poor impression on an audience.

If you plan to use the blackboard, you don't have to worry so much about your drawings being attractive. No one expects blackboard work to be beautiful. Make the drawings large and dark so that they can be seen easily, and plan them in advance so that you have a chance to try out various formats and pick the clearest one. When you give the speech, do your blackboard drawing or writing *while* you are talking. Long pauses lose audience attention. If what you plan to do is too complex to put on the board while you are talking, put it on cards or charts in advance and show them at appropriate times. The great appeal of blackboard work is its immediacy. If you can draw or write and talk at the same time, it can have great impact.

PRACTICE

Follow the suggestions given in the preceding assignment. In addition, you will need to practice placing and handling your visual aids. Plan their placement so that they will be handy for your use and clearly visible to the audience. You may want some of them to be visible during the whole speech and others to be concealed until you are ready to present them. To hide cards or charts, you can turn them to the wall or put a blank card or piece of paper over the top one. To hide objects, you can put them in a box or drape some material over them. A collection of interesting-looking objects in full view while you are talking about something else will distract the audience, so keep "permanent exhibits" to a minimum and bring most aids out only when you are ready to discuss them.

Practice the handling of your visual aids and all movement that relates to them so you can use them with poise and control. Figure out how to set up the aids rapidly and efficiently before you begin talking. You don't want to look disorganized or rushed, but you don't want to waste time either. Time your use of aids to fit the vocal delivery of your explanatory material. Careful planning is needed here to make your presentation smooth. It is not easy to juggle several elements, but it should *look* easy.

DELIVERY

Review the suggestions given for delivery in your last assignment. In addition, be sure that you talk to your audience, not to your visual aids. Face the audience as much of the time as you can. When you point to your aids, do it briefly, and then look squarely at your audience while giving your explanation. Keep checking sight lines: can the whole audience see both you and the visual aids? When you come to a part of the speech in which you are not using prepared aids or the blackboard, move away from them and toward the audience. This simple movement reminds the audience that it is them you are really interested in, not the aids, and makes you a much more compelling speaker.

During the speech, project the confidence that comes from control of yourself, your material, and your audience. Confidence and modesty *do* go together. Communicate your enthusiasm in gesture, word, and vocal inflection, and confess your own problems in learning about your subject. You need to show the audience that you know what you're doing and wish to share your knowledge with them, and also that you want to help them avoid the mistakes you have made.

CRITICISM

Review and follow the suggestions given in the last assignment.

SAMPLE STUDENT OUTLINE

INTRODUCTION

I Building or buying a home represents one of the largest financial transactions of a lifetime for the average family and can be the happy conclusion of many years of planning and saving.

  A. There is always the possibility of not getting your money's worth.

  B. An error in judgment in purchasing a house cannot simply be charged off to experience.

  C. The consequences of bad judgment could be a serious or even critical financial loss.

II I would like to save some of you future home-owners from making those bad judgments by pointing out some things to think about in buying a house.

BODY

I The selection of the right site has an important influence on home planning and on the welfare of your family.

  A. Once you think you are ready to buy a house, take a look at the community you might like to live in.

    1. Do you want to live in a rich community?

    2. Are the homes well kept?

    3. Are there stores near by?

    4. Is there adequate fire and police protection?

    5. Are the schools within walking distance of the home?

    6. Is the church of your choice reasonably near?

    7. Are there adequate recreational facilities?

  B. Let's take a look at the plot itself.

    1. Is it large enough for what you want?

    2. Does it face the direction you desire?

      a) Will you get the summer breezes?

      b) Might you want the backyard in full sun so that some day you can have a swimming pool and the sun will heat it?

II Finding a plan suitable for your family is very important.

    A. Since the housewife spends the greater part of her day performing household duties, a well-planned house should provide her freedom from drudgery.

        1. Most housework is done from the kitchen.

            a) The kitchen should be centrally located.

            b) This will save steps and unnecessary work.

            c) Adequate eating space in the kitchen saves much work in serving meals.

        2. The housewife should be able to see the children playing outside from the kitchen window.

        3. There should be adequate storage.

            a) I once saw a tract house in this area which had not one single linen closet.

            b) A house needs many cupboards.

        4. A laundry room next to the kitchen will save many steps.

    B. Privacy and quiet are essential requirements of the sleeping area of the house.

        1. The bathroom should be accessible to all the bedrooms so that people can reach it without disturbing those who are already asleep.

            a) The bath should be easy to reach from all bedrooms.

            b) The bath should be easy to reach from main entry.

        2. The bedroom should be large enough to allow you to make the beds without bumping into other furniture.

            a) Notice how small some of the bedrooms are in some of the housing tracts in this area.

            b) You may need room for a desk or bookcase.

        3. A bedroom should have good cross-ventilation.

    C. The best overall plan for a house is one in which it is possible to go into any room in the house without going through another, or at least not much of another.

        1. Let's see what is wrong with this plan.

            a) The porch lacks privacy.

b) A visitor at the front door can view the entire living and dining rooms and even see into the kitchen

c) The living room is small and cut up, making the furniture arrangement difficult.

d) The dining room has too many doors.

e) The kitchen is poorly arranged.

f) There are two doors to the bathroom, so for privacy two doors have to be secured.

g) Guests have to go through a bedroom to use the bath.

h) The bedroom near the kitchen is too small even to make the bed.

2. Now let's look at this plan, which has the same amount of space as the first but is much better arranged.

a) The front door swings against a screen, forming a vestibule.

b) The living room is much easier to arrange.

c) The dining room is part of the living room and is thus more usable.

d) Traffic bypasses the dining room table.

e) The porch offers a view of the backyard.

f) The kitchen and bath share the plumbing, so it is less costly to build.

g) The bath is easily accessible.

h) The bedrooms are better arranged.

3. This plan won the Sunset Award for 1967.

a) Notice how one can go to either the living area or the bedroom area without disturbing anyone.

b) The walled court gives privacy and protection for the children.

4. This plan is from *Better Homes and Gardens*, September issue.

a) The plan is very similar to the Sunset house, only bigger.

b) The square footage of this house is 2,250, and in the Sunset house it was 1,560 square feet.

CONCLUSION

I Now that I have shown you some things to look for in site selection and plans, I hope you all do better than my husband and I did on our first house.

    A. For nineteen years I lived in a house hearing my mother constantly complaining that as she sat down at the dining room table she looked directly into the bathroom with a great view of the toilet.

    B. You guessed it—we bought our first house thinking we had checked everything and the first time we sat down at the dining room table you know what view I had!

BIBLIOGRAPHY

Kenneth B. Johnstone et al., Building or Buying a House. New York and London: McGraw-Hill Book Company, Inc., 1945.

Sunset, October 1967.

Better Homes and Gardens, September 1967.

QUESTIONS FOR DISCUSSION

1. What specific audience interest is developed in the Introduction?

2. What are the main points? Does each relate clearly to the purpose? Are they parallel?

3. What is the major method of development in the body of the speech, under 1 A and B?

4. Where has the speaker used her own experience?

5. Is there enough specific material to assist you if you were going to buy or build a home? What specific information in the speech would be most helpful?

6. If you were going to make this speech, what kinds of visual aids would you use and why?

7. Where does the speaker give credit to her research sources?

8. Is a summary given in the conclusion? Is one needed?

9. What is effective about the ending of the speech?

OUTLINE: COMMUNICATING WITH VISUAL AIDS

Subject:

Topic:

INTRODUCTION

1 Attention device

2 Need

3 Thesis

OUTLINE: COMMUNICATING WITH VISUAL AIDS

BODY

Main points (not less than two or more than five; parallel in wording; clearly related to each other and to your purpose) and support for each point

OUTLINE: COMMUNICATING WITH VISUAL AIDS

CONCLUSION

1 Summary

2 Closing appeal

OUTLINE: COMMUNICATING WITH VISUAL AIDS

3 Bibliography

CHECK LIST FOR ORIGINALITY

1. Have I used my own experience wherever possible?
2. Have I put the material in my own words?
3. Have I used research material from several sources?
4. Have I given proper credit for quoted material?
5. Are the conclusions my own and based on careful research and thought?

OUTLINE: COMMUNICATING WITH VISUAL AIDS

Subject:

Topic:

INTRODUCTION

1 Attention device

2 Need

3 Thesis

OUTLINE: COMMUNICATING WITH VISUAL AIDS

BODY

Main points (not less than two or more than five; parallel in wording; clearly related to each other and to your purpose) and support for each point

OUTLINE: COMMUNICATING WITH VISUAL AIDS

CONCLUSION

1 Summary

2 Closing appeal

OUTLINE: COMMUNICATING WITH VISUAL AIDS

3 Bibliography

CHECK LIST FOR ORIGINALITY

1. Have I used my own experience wherever possible?
2. Have I put the material in my own words?
3. Have I used research material from several sources?
4. Have I given proper credit for quoted material?
5. Are the conclusions my own and based on careful research and thought?

INSTRUCTOR'S EVALUATION:
COMMUNICATING WITH VISUAL AIDS

1 Delivery

   A. Voice

   B. Enthusiasm

   C. Posture

   D. Appearance

   E. Gestures

   F. Eye contact

   G. Movement

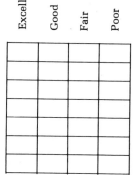

2 Material

   A. Introduction

       1. Attention step

       2. Need step

       3. Thesis

   B. Body

       1. Main points

       2. Development

   C. Conclusion

       1. Summary

       2. Closing appeal

   D. Transitions

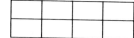

(Rating columns: Excellent, Good, Fair, Poor)

INSTRUCTOR'S EVALUATION:
COMMUNICATING WITH VISUAL AIDS

	Excellent	Good	Fair	Poor

3 Language
   A. Vocabulary
   B. Sentence Structure

	Excellent	Good	Fair	Poor

4 Visual Aids
   A. Setting up
   B. Handling
   C. Timing of aids with speech
   D. Visibility
   E. Clarity

	Excellent	Good	Fair	Poor

5 Comments

GRADE _____   INSTRUCTOR _____

6

COMMUNICATING
WITH ANECDOTES

As you have already seen in Chapter 3, Telling Your Experience to Make a Point, personal experience in the form of anecdotes is often the most interesting and valuable support you can have for your opinions and judgments.

One very effective type of speaking is the expository speech based largely on personal experience or observations and developed through the use of anecdotes. The anecdotes (or detailed illustrations) clarify and emphasize the expository points; they also present the speaker's "credentials," show what he is like as a person, and move or entertain the audience.

I remember an occasion on which I was asked to discuss the problems of our department in five minutes. This seemed to me an impossible task, since there were several problems, each of which would take five minutes to explain adequately! I began my speech with the following anecdote:

> Thinking about the assigned topic and time limit reminds me of a story about Winston Churchill, who was invited to speak at a meeting of a women's temperance society. Churchill was, of course, surprised, because he was not known for his temperance. At the meeting he was introduced as a horrible example of intemperance. The introduction ended with the charge that "The alcoholic beverages that Mr. Churchill has consumed would half fill this room!" Churchill stood up and during a thoughtful pause mentally examined the dimensions of the large hall and then began with, "So much to do—and so little time!"

The anecdote was effective as an attention device, but, in addition, I was able in an indirect and humorous way to make my feelings about the assignment clear. You may also observe that the Churchill anecdote as given above is an anecdote within an anecdote about my personal experience as a speaker.

In an article on violence, one writer effectively developed his ideas about psychological violence with the following explanation and anecdote:

> The overt forms of violence are, on the whole, easier to recognize than quiet or covert violence, which does not necessarily involve direct physical assault on anybody's person or property. There are both personal and institutional forms of quiet violence. Consider first a case of what we might call psychological violence, involving individuals. The following item appeared in *The New York Times:*
>
> PHOENIX, Ariz., Feb. 6 (AP)—Linda Marie Ault killed herself, policemen said today, rather than make her dog Beauty pay for her night with a married man.
>
> The police quoted her parents, Mr. and Mrs. Joseph Ault, as giving this account:
>
> Linda failed to return home from a dance in Tempe Friday night. On Saturday she admitted she had spent the night with an Air Force lieutenant.
>
> The Aults decided on a punishment that would "wake Linda up." They ordered her to shoot the dog she had owned about two years.
>
> On Sunday, the Aults and Linda took the dog into the desert near their home. They had the girl dig a shallow grave. Then Mrs. Ault grasped the dog between her hands, and Mr. Ault gave his daughter a .22-caliber pistol and told her to shoot the dog.
>
> Instead, the girl put the pistol to her right temple and shot herself.
>
> The police said there were no charges that could be filed against the parents except possible cruelty to animals.
>
> The reason there can be no charges is that the parents did no physical damage to Linda. But that they did terrible violence to the girl the father himself recognized when he said to a detective, "I killed her; I killed her. It's just like I killed her myself." If we fail to recognize that a real psychological violence can be perpetrated on people, a violation of their autonomy, their dignity, their right to determine things for themselves, to be men rather than dogs, then we fail to realize the full dimension of what it is to do violence.*

The anecdote given in the news item was particularly effective because it not only clarified what the author meant by showing it in terms of real human behavior, but it made us *feel* the "full dimension" of this kind of violence.

The first time you are called upon to speak to a club or organization, try giving this kind of speech. It's an almost sure-fire method of exposition.

---

*Newton Carver, "What Violence Is," *The Nation*, June 24, 1968.

ASSIGNMENT

Select a subject with which you have had a great deal of personal experience, perhaps through jobs you have held or hobbies or special interests you enjoy, and plan to use anecdotes to present it to your class.

SUBJECT

Any will do. Many people feel that some subjects are naturally interesting and some are naturally dull, but this isn't really true. You can make any subject interesting for any audience, if you plan the purpose and the material with that audience in mind. The important thing in this assignment is that you select a subject with which you have a great deal of personal experience, so that you can use your experiences in developing the speech.

TOPIC

After you have chosen a subject, narrow it down to a topic by asking what aspect of the subject is most appropriate for your particular audience. Think over everything you know about your subject and everything you know about your audience. Go back if necessary and review your listening notes from the introductory speeches given by members of the class. Then ask yourself three questions: What aspect of the subject should the audience be introduced to first? What aspect of the subject is most dramatic or striking? What aspect would have the greatest practical value for your audience?

Any one of these questions can lead you to a suitable audience-centered topic. For example, if you are an education major and you wish to talk about college students, your answer to the first question might be "kinds of college students"; your answer to the second question might be "reasons that college students commit suicide"; and your answer to the third question might be "how to get a scholarship." Any one of these would be a good topic, with real interest for your audience. When you try the procedure with your own subject, list several topics in answer to each question and then select the one from your list that you and your audience will enjoy most.

THESIS

Follow the directions given in your last assignment for writing a thesis statement. Then apply these tests for a good thesis:
1. Is it brief? If your sentence is long and rambling, you probably

97

don't have your purpose clearly in mind and your audience will not be able to grasp it.

2. Does it contain one idea? If your thesis is a compound or a complex sentence containing more than one idea, your speech will probably lack unity. Unity means oneness, and to have it your speech must develop one clear purpose.

3. Does it indicate exactly what I plan to cover? "I want to discuss with you four major causes of the Civil War" is a good thesis statement; "I want to tell you a little about the Civil War" and "I want to tell you what I know about the Civil War" are poor ones. The phrases "a little about" and "what I know about" are too vague and general—they will mean nothing to the audience. Be suspicious any time you find yourself using the word *about* in your thesis statement. It may mean that you have not defined your topic clearly in your own mind.

MAIN POINTS

Follow the directions given in your last assignment for planning your main points. Be sure that they are parallel in wording and clearly related to each other and to your purpose.

If you have trouble writing your main points, something may be wrong with your thesis statement. A good statement of purpose frequently dictates the organization of a speech and makes the main points easy to write. If you are talking about kinds of college students, each main point will be a kind; if you are talking about reasons college students commit suicide, each main point will be a reason; if you are talking about how to get a scholarship, each main point will be a method (or step, depending on your approach).

DEVELOPMENT

The key to developing an interesting speech is human interest. All people are not interested in all topics, but all people are interested in people. If you can talk about your topic in terms of human behavior, you can count on a high degree of interest from all your listeners.

Test this generalization by using an anecdote (from your own experience if possible) under each main point. If your topic is kinds of college students, under each kind tell a story about some experience you had with that kind of student; if your topic is reasons that college students commit suicide, under each reason tell about a student who committed suicide for that reason; if your topic is how to get a scholarship, under each method tell about a student who got a scholarship by using that method. Although one example is not enough to develop a point fully (you need to mention additional examples, even though you do not develop them in detail, to show that your example is not an isolated case), a carefully chosen anecdote will do much to support and clarify your point at the same time that it adds human interest to the speech.

Develop each anecdote the same way you developed your story in Chapter 3, Telling Your Experience to Make a Point. Remember that your anecdotes can suggest a great deal about you as a person. What specific things do you want to suggest? How will you suggest them?

When you define and explain unfamiliar words and activities, consider the technique of comparing the unfamiliar to the familiar: "Riding a motorcycle is like riding a bike and driving a car at the same time." This is a good, clear technique; the only danger is that it can sound condescending. Be careful not to assume an air of superiority because you know this material and your audience does not. Instead of saying or implying, "You don't know this, so I'll explain it to you," try saying something like, "When I first heard about X, it was explained to me this way." If visual aids are appropriate to your topic, use them.

During your speech, give credit at appropriate times to the sources you used in researching your subject. If it seems appropriate, include a direct quotation from each source. This procedure gives authority to the development of your topic and also shows that you are a responsible person who has researched his topic thoroughly and gives credit where credit is due.

Address the audience directly, using the pronons *I*, *we*, and *you* liberally, to show your listeners that your whole speech has been planned with them in mind. A good rule of thumb is to use *you* for compliments ("you did this well") and *we* for criticisms ("we have failed"). Anecdotes go well with a direct, informal presentation, so feel free to refer to members of your audience by name and to mention specific interests you know they have. This shows that you are aware of your listeners as individuals, and that you have paid attention to what they have told the class. It also holds the group together by reminding them of common experiences.

Plan to use an anecdote in the introduction of your speech as well as under each main point. The introductory anecdote may indicate how you became interested in your topic, or how you came to select it for this audience or this occasion. In either event, the purpose is to get audience attention, to introduce your subject, and to show the audience that you have their best interests at heart. If you cannot use a personal experience, relate one you have heard or read about. After the anecdote, emphasize the importance of your topic to your audience and announce your purpose.

In your conclusion, summarize the body of your speech and make an appeal for action. The appeal should be related to the audience interest developed throughout the speech.

Analyze the sample outline at the end of this chapter. Then make two copies of the outline for your speech on the forms provided. Give one outline to your instructor, with the blank evaluation form provided for his or her use, and keep the other outline for your own use in practicing and delivering the speech.

PRACTICE

Follow the suggestions given for rehearsing your previous assignments. Work for fluency and control in your explanatory passages and for spontaneity and informality in your anecdotes. The variation in tone as you move from explanation to anecdote and back to explanation again will help emphasize important ideas and hold audience attention, and it will offer your listeners a little relaxation so that they will be mentally refreshed for each new main point.

DELIVERY

Follow the suggestions given in your last two assignments. In addition, try changing your physical position when you change the tone of your speech. For example, stand behind the speaker's stand in an alert, erect posture when you deliver the expository passages; for your anecdotes, move out from behind the stand, closer to your audience, and adopt a more relaxed attitude (perhaps resting an arm on the side of the speaker's stand). When another expository passage comes up, return to your previous position. These physical actions reinforce changes in the tone of the material.

CRITICISM

As the members of the class give their talks, take notes on the forms described in Chapter 13. Give the forms to the appropriate speakers. After you have given your own speech and collected the evaluation forms, determine what seem to be your strengths and your weaknesses as your listeners see them, using the summary sheets on pages 113–115.

Then make a plan for improvement. Do you need to speak louder? use more gestures and facial expressions? spend more time on research? make more detailed outlines? work harder on a clear organization pattern? In future assignments, give special attention to specific areas in which you want to improve.

SAMPLE STUDENT OUTLINE

INTRODUCTION

I *Attention statement.* What do you think of your dreams? Are they amusing? Frightening? Baffling? Most people experience all three of these reactions to their mysterious nighttime fantasies.

II *Transition.* Throughout the ages, man has wondered about dreams. Almost every people indicated belief in the meaningfulness of dreams. The combined findings of centuries of dream interpretation were summarized by Artemidorus in the second century A.D. During the centuries that followed, it is said by some that dreams became better defined, though the authority behind them was open to question. While scientific research has been a great help in many fields of endeavor, it has led to confusion in the field of dreams. Man has learned very little about dreams in the past few thousand years.

III *Thesis.* Let us examine the theory of Artemidorus, one of the most systematic theories of dream interpretation ever developed.

IV *Preview of main points.* According to Artemidorus, there are five different kinds of dreams. The first is a True Dream, the second a Vision, the third an Oracle, the fourth a Phantasy, and the fifth an Apparition.

BODY

I In a *True Dream* according to his definition, one may see events that in somewhat disguised form present the truth of the world as we know it. Anecdote: Pharaoh's dream.

II *Vision* he defined as the appearance of someone, the seeing of someone exactly the way this person is known to look when examined by a nonsleeping person. Anecdote: Dream of my husband wearing shoes of two colors.

III An *Oracle* is a divine revelation sent while we are sleeping in order to inform us of some matter of great importance. Anecdote: Dream of Joseph, husband of the Virgin Mary.

IV A *Phantasy* brings us in our sleep the images of persons or things we have been longing for. Anecdote: Dream of hunger for food and water.

V An *Apparition* is a vision, seen at night, which fills us with horror. Today we call it a nightmare. Anecdote: Dream of my daughter and the snakes.

CONCLUSION

I *Summary.* The True Dream, the Vision, the Oracle, the Apparition, and the Phantasy are the five different kinds of dreams of the Artemidorus theory. This is a theory of only one man who worked many years on dream investigations. There have been other theories and there will be many more in the future.

II *Closing interest.* We hope, through further research, we will discover the full meaning of dreams.

BIBLIOGRAPHY

Erich Fromm, *The Forgotten Language.* New York: Rinehart & Co., Inc., 1959.

C. G. Jung, *The Basic Writing of C. G. Jung.* New York: The Modern Library, 1959.

Joseph L. Morse, "Joseph and Mary," *Encyclopaedia Britannica*, XXI, 440–41, 1953.

André Sonnet, *The Twilight Zone of Dreams,* New York: Chilton Co., 1961.

QUESTIONS FOR DISCUSSION

1. The main points are not parallel. Rewrite them to make them parallel.

2. What audience interest is developed throughout the speech? Where does it first appear? Where does it last appear?

3. This outline has less detail than previous sample outlines. Do you think more detail is needed? Why or why not?

4. Each main point is explained and then developed with one anecdote. Is one sufficient?

5. Where has the speaker used her own experience?

6. Is there a summary? Is one needed?

7. Where are the sources credited in the material of the speech?

8. If you were giving this speech, would you use visual aids? If not, why not? If so, what kind and why?

OUTLINE: COMMUNICATING WITH ANECDOTES

Subject:

Topic:

INTRODUCTION

1 Attention device

2 Need

3 Thesis

OUTLINE: COMMUNICATING WITH ANECDOTES

BODY

Main points (not less than two or more than five; parallel in wording; clearly related to each other and to your purpose) and support for each point

OUTLINE: COMMUNICATING WITH ANECDOTES

CONCLUSION

1 Summary

2 Closing appeal

OUTLINE: COMMUNICATING WITH ANECDOTES

3 Bibliography

CHECK LIST FOR DEVELOPING AUDIENCE INTEREST

1. Have I used appropriate and vivid anecdotes to illustrate all my points?
2. Have I planned all sentences with the audience in mind and used pronouns (I, we, you) to show that this is the case?
3. Is the purpose of my speech based on an interest or need of my audience?
4. Is that interest or need developed and referred to throughout the speech?
5. Does my speech clearly show my feelings as well as my ideas?

OUTLINE: COMMUNICATING WITH ANECDOTES

Subject:

Topic:

INTRODUCTION

1 Attention device

2 Need

3 Thesis

OUTLINE: COMMUNICATING WITH ANECDOTES

BODY

Main points (not less than two or more than five; parallel in wording; clearly related to each other and to your purpose) and support for each point

OUTLINE: COMMUNICATING WITH ANECDOTES

CONCLUSION

1 Summary

2 Closing appeal

OUTLINE: COMMUNICATING WITH ANECDOTES

3 Bibliography

CHECK LIST FOR DEVELOPING AUDIENCE INTEREST

1. Have I used appropriate and vivid anecdotes to illustrate all my points?
2. Have I planned all sentences with the audience in mind and used pronouns (I, we, you) to show that this is the case?
3. Is the purpose of my speech based on an interest or need of my audience?
4. Is that interest or need developed and referred to throughout the speech?
5. Does my speech clearly show my feelings as well as my ideas?

INSTRUCTOR'S EVALUATION:

COMMUNICATING WITH ANECDOTES

	Excellent	Good	Fair	Poor

1 Delivery

   A. Voice

   B. Enthusiasm

   C. Posture

   D. Appearance

   E. Gestures

   F. Eye contact

   G. Movement

2 Material

   A. Introduction

      1. Attention step

      2. Need step

      3. Thesis

   B. Body

      1. Main points

      2. Development

   C. Conclusion

      1. Summary

      2. Closing appeal

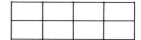

   D. Transitions

INSTRUCTOR'S EVALUATION:

COMMUNICATING WITH ANECDOTES

	Excellent	Good	Fair	Poor

3 Language
   A. Vocabulary
   B. Sentence structure

4 Anecdotes
   A. Use of speaker's own experience
   B. Suitability of anecdotes to material
   C. Suitability of anecdotes to audience
   D. Development of emotional impact
   E. Selection of detail to make points clear

5 Comments

GRADE _____ INSTRUCTOR _____

SUMMARY OF CRITICISMS:

COMMUNICATING WITH ANECDOTES

Number of Times
Mentioned

1 Strengths
   Most critics mentioned these:

   Many critics mentioned these:

   A few critics mentioned these:

SUMMARY OF CRITICISMS:

COMMUNICATING WITH ANECDOTES

Number of Times
Mentioned

2 Weaknesses
Most critics mentioned these:

Many critics mentioned these:

A few critics mentioned these:

SUMMARY OF CRITICISMS:

COMMUNICATING WITH ANECDOTES

3 Specific areas that need improvement

3
COMMUNICATING TO PERSUADE

You have a responsibility to share your convictions as well as your knowledge with others. Ideas that you think are true or false, actions that you think lead to happiness or misery—it is important to communicate your convictions on such matters, whether others agree with you or not. Knowing what you feel strongly about will help people know you, and it will also help them understand the world they live in by showing them how someone else interprets it. Only by examining all the alternatives can we select the best answers.

Your assignments in this section will ask you to be honest with yourself about what you believe, to communicate your convictions honestly to others, and to be open-minded in considering beliefs that are different from your own. You must evaluate your convictions, and with them the knowledge on which they are based. If your knowledge is spotty, do some research, including observation and interviewing. Along with the facts that back up your beliefs, **remember to communicate yourself**—your experiences, your reservations, your personality. Beliefs are partly based on fact, but they are also very personal things. Your listeners need to know you in order to evaluate your ideas fairly for themselves.

Communicating your convictions to others will increase your understanding of who you are and what you believe as well as your capacity for giving to others. Understanding why you feel as you do will help you understand why others feel as they do, which makes possible closer personal relationships and a genuine exchange of ideas.

REVENUERS AND OTHER THUGS

MURRAY N. ROTHBARD

Murray N. Rothbard is Professor of Economics at the New York Polytechnic Institute and editor of the *Libertarian Forum*. His article presents some highly controversial ideas on a topic of importance to all of us—income tax. Read it through carefully and critically. It may suggest topics that would be suitable for your own speeches. Later on, you will be asked to reread it and to analyze it, using the discussion questions that follow it, in order to help you complete the assignments in Chapters 8 and 9.

Every individual, group, organization and institution in society gets income in one of two ways: either through voluntary purchase by users or consumers of its goods and services, or through voluntary contributions by members or donors. In either case, the payment of money is optional, reflecting either a desire to buy the organization's product or to advance its activity. There is, of course, an exception: theft. The thief or robber gets *his* income, not by voluntary purchase or gift, but by forcing funds from his victim through violence or the threat of violence. The thief gains his income at the expense of his victims.

There is another glaring exception to this social rule of voluntary payment and income. That exception is *government*, which obtains its revenue (called "taxes") in precisely the same way; taxation is a compulsory levy that no person or institution is allowed to consider or reject. Just as the holdup man obtains his revenue by threatening harm to anyone who might dare refuse, so the government threatens further confiscation and ultimately imprisonment should anyone refuse to pay (and further violence should the victim "resist arrest").

The point, then, is that there is no difference between taxation and robbery. Since any organization that systematically employs robbery to obtain its income is defined as a criminal organization, we must conclude that government—*all* government—is an organization of robbers. If anyone should balk at this startling idea, I challenge him to sit down and try to work out a definition of robbery that does not *also* apply to taxation. For what else is the compulsory extraction of funds, with violence employed if demands are not met?

There are, of course, many social differences, but they stem not from a real distinction in action, but from contrasting social *attitudes* toward the two kinds of payment and organization. No magazine would ever publish a symposium on whether robbery is a good or a bad thing, whether it should be abolished or fostered. Virtually everyone despises crime; the only arguments revolve about *how* crime can be reduced or eliminated. Even the mightiest criminal syndicate lacks sympathy or legitimacy in the eyes of the public, and it is always on the run. Such is scarcely true of government. On the contrary, government officials generally enjoy high status in the community, and their extortions are hailed as essential to the "common good," the "general welfare," and the "public interest." Such has been the success of the massive propaganda campaign conducted by governments over the centuries.

Government conducts its robberies on a much grander scale than any group of acknowledged criminals. Far from being on the run, its leaders are revered, sometimes even thought of as sovereigns. Another distinction is that ordinary robbers, whatever else they may be, aren't hypocrites. They don't pretend that they are robbing a victim for his benefit, or that the robber's spending will stabilize the economy, create jobs and add to society's purchasing power. No robber would have the bad taste or the gall to justify his acts in that way; the gall and the arguments are reserved to the organizers and apologists for government.

Another reason the simple robber is more decent and less despotic than government is that after robbing you, he at least has the good grace to *leave you alone*. The government, far from leaving you alone, is always at your side, insisting on annual compulsory tribute, calling itself your "sovereign," ordering you to salute its battle flag and forcing you to fight for it when it wishes to conduct battles against rival gangs in remote climes. And to make sure that you and future generations will put up with this system without much complaint, it forces your children into its "educational" centers where it promotes the virtues of obedience to its authority. Furthermore, the robber confines himself to spending his ill-gotten gains on his own private consumption. The government, while of course doing the same, also spends a large portion of its loot on propagandizing us on its behalf and, what is more, on forcing us to act in ways *it* considers moral. Think of it. Society's mightiest and most hypocritical collection of gangsters has managed to allot to itself the role of guardian of the public's "morality." No Mafioso would ever contemplate behaving with such colossal effrontery.

Once one realizes that taxation is organized theft, the social and economic effects become clear. For the state exists as a parasite upon both producers and consumers. The greater the tax load, the lower the standard of living of the producers, and the lower the incentive for producers to continue working and saving. As in every kind of parasitism, the host body is less and less able to produce for itself as the parasite grows fat; if the parasite does too much blood sucking, the host dies, and so then the parasite. Such will be our fate if the tax burden on production becomes too great.

Much ink has been spilled on arguing what *form* taxation should take: whether it should be "progressive" (taxing the rich) or "regressive" (taxing the poor or the middle class). By arguing about *who* should be robbed we divert attention from the fundamental issue: whether *any* robbery should take place. It is both immoral and oppressive to tax the poor, who are only made poorer by the depredation, but it is equally immoral and economically destructive to tax the rich, whose saving and investment are particularly taxed. Progressive taxation is simply the old highwayman's practice of extracting money from the most promising targets.

There is another neglected point that should be made about progressive income taxation. Most people think that it taxes "the rich." What it really does is to tax not those who have capital but those who currently are earning income. It taxes not so much those who are *already* rich, as those who are trying to *become* rich. In short, progressive income taxation injures those who are successfully trying to compete with the current rich, and thus impedes mobility and the ability of people to better their lot.

As government has grown in our society, however, it has found that there aren't enough rich people, and so the poor and the middle class are taxed heavily too. Conservatives who oppose progressive taxation in our day have their priorities wrong; it is not the poor who are robbing the rich, but the government that is robbing both, and every income group in between. The "welfare state," like the other slogans of government, is nothing but a racket. Two examples will suffice. Herriott and Miller (writing in *The Conference Board Record*, May 1971) have estimated that people in 1968 making less than $2,000 a year paid, on the average, 50 percent of their income in taxes of all kinds, while those making $50,000 a year and more paid 45 percent of their income in taxes. A fascinating study was made by Earl Mellor for the Institute for Policy Studies of the money paid to the federal government in taxes, compared to the money paid out by the government, in fiscal year 1967, in the low-income mixed race area of Shaw-Cardozo in Washington, D.C. The money flowing into the area from the government, ranging from welfare benefits to expenditures on public schools, was estimated at $45.7 million. But the total outflow of taxes from Shaw-Cardozo came to $50.0 million, a net out-flow from the low-income neighborhood of $4.3 million *to* the government. So much for the "welfare state," which is welfare not so much for the poor, as for public officials and the other recipients of government's largess and subsidies.

If we take a close look at the salaries of government officials we will see that in fact they pay *no taxes at all*. Tax payments by bureaucrats are an accounting fiction, designed to gull the unfortunate tax-paying public. Suppose that a bureaucrat makes $30,000 a year, and pays $10,000 in taxes; in actual fact, he is not a net taxpayer at all, but a net "tax consumer" (to use the happy phrase of John C. Calhoun 150 years ago). He is really living off your taxes and mine to the tune of $20,000.

As Calhoun also pointed out, in a world where taxation was minimal, the very existence of taxation sets up two mighty and conflicting classes in society: the net taxpayers, and the net tax consumers. The latter live off the former group. As the tax burden grows, the class conflict in society is aggravated, for it becomes ever more important for persons to join the tax consumer group and to escape the ranks of the burdened taxpayers. The scramble to get funds from the government trough accelerates, and class conflict, not just the burden of parasitism on the economy, intensifies.

Of all the forms of taxation, the worst and most oppressive is the income tax, but not primarily because the income tax is more or less "progressive" than other taxes (although no other tax can single out and loot the rich *and* the poor in quite as effective and drastic a way). The main evil of the income tax is that it provides a method by which the government pries into the lives and actions of every citizen in the country. No one is safe from the legalized spying of the Internal Revenue Service. We now know the IRS files have been used by whatever regime happened to be in power to harass political dissidents. The income tax is the single most oppressive institution in modern life.

It is a good thing that despite centuries of persistent propaganda the average citizen has an intuitive perception of the truth that taxation is robbery, and that the income tax is the major culprit. Most people think it's immoral to cheat friends, neighbors and business associates. Yet, how many people consider it *immoral* to cheat on their income tax returns? Even now, income-tax cheating and evasion is endemic; the only thing that inhibits it is not moral qualms but the perfectly sensible fear of getting caught. As H. L. Mencken wrote 50 years ago:

> When a private citizen is robbed a worthy man is deprived of the fruits of industry and thrift; when the government is robbed the worst that happens is that certain rogues and loafers have less money to play with than they had before. The notion that they have earned that money is never entertained; to most sensible men it would seem ludicrous. They are simply rascals who, by accidents of law, have a somewhat dubious right to a share in the earnings of their fellow men.

Yet the myth propounded by political scientists, economists and other apologists for government is that taxation is "really" voluntary, that the people freely decide to pay taxes in return for the numerous "services" the government performs.

In contrast, the great economist Joseph Schumpeter chided:

> . . . ever since the princes' feudal incomes ceased to be of major importance, the State has been living on a revenue which was being produced in the private sphere for private purposes and had to be deflected from these purposes by political force. The theory which construes taxes on the analogy of club dues or of the purchase of services of, say, a doctor, only proves how far removed this part of the social sciences is from scientific habits of mind.

All right, there is an easy way to settle this dispute, a way that would also have the incidental benefit of removing the parasitic blight of organized robbery from our social and economic life. Let us try a noble experiment: let all levels of government—federal, state and local—remove compulsion from the tax system. Let them repeal all the penalties for nonpayment of taxes. Let the various governments issue requests for funds, let them put the public on the "honor system" and convert taxes to the status of donations to the Salvation Army, and let them see what happens. Let us see how much revenue would then flow freely to the coffers of government. I would predict very little, while presumably the apologists for our tax system would say that government revenues would be sustained at almost the current level. Let's find out. And, as we find out, we will also remove the criminality from government's inflow of funds, and convert government to the status of every other social institution whose income is a voluntary expression of consumer or donor support. The people would then be supporting only that level of government that they truly *wish* to support.

If people voluntarily pay only a small sum to government, wouldn't that mean a drastic reduction in the supply of government services they enjoy? Yes, but it would also mean that the people *prefer* to spend their own earnings on the other goods and services that they enjoy in the private sector. Why not let us—the people—make our own choices with the fruits of our own work and energy? To say otherwise, to endorse the government's power to coerce people into paying its revenue, is to enshrine the principle of dictatorship and despotism and to violate the essential principles of individual freedom and cooperation that are the glories of America's heritage.

In fact, of the services government supposedly provides, many are services only in the sense of a grisly jest. Robbery and compulsion serve us ill. Controls and regulations prevent us from doing what we want to do with our own lives and property; coerced "morality" prevents all of us from making our own moral choices and decisions. And those services that government *does* perform it renders badly and inefficiently, as does any coercive monopolist (that is, anyone who has a government license to perform a service free from competition). Clearly, for example, delivery of the mail is vital to all of us. But how does the federal government perform the service? By giving its own post office a legal monopoly to deliver first class mail, with no legal private competition. Not only does such a monopolist perform as we might expect (steadily rising rates and lower quality service), it also creates a haven for politics and inefficiency. It subsidizes one type of mail at the expense of others, and even presumes to control the *kind* of mail we send by restricting or outlawing pornographic mail, and by agreeing to allow federal agencies to open or monitor the mail of political dissenters. No private mail deliverers would ever treat their customers with such contempt, a contempt strengthened by the fact that the postal service covers its eternal deficits by dipping into the tax till.

The example of the post office can be extended to all of the other services provided and monopolized by the government. Each one of them could be supplied far more efficiently, far more cheaply and far more morally, by the free competition of private businesses in a free market. Only in a totally free market can consumers decide how to spend their income, and how much of each service to purchase, or to contribute to out of their earnings. It is only a totally free and unhampered market, a market free of the burden of taxation-theft, that can determine how resources are to be allocated for the maximum benefit of the consumers, while leaving all of us uncoerced in the process.

How could the free market supply essential services that we have come to think of as uniquely governmental? No one can blueprint the market in advance, for there is no way to predict, in any particular industry, what forms creative energy will take, or what will be profitable. But some broad prognoses can be made. In the case of the postal service, the task is easy; for with the disappearance of the lumbering postal monopoly, competing firms will leap into the breach to fulfill the demands of the consumers. During the 19th century, when the U.S. government allowed private competition in the postal service, private mail deliverers lowered the price of mail and pioneered in innovations in postal service. Consider the more complex case of fire fighting. If government fire departments were eliminated, there might be a return to the older system—still in force in many small towns today—of volunteer fire fighting teams drawn from the community. In the larger cities volunteerism is inefficient; paid, professional fire fighters are needed to provide round-the-clock service. In that case, fire fighting companies would spring up in the market, charging a fee for their services. To obviate the problem of paying per fire, most homeowners and landlords could pay a monthly or annual premium, putting the fire fighters on a retainer basis. In short, fire service would be paid for in the manner of insurance, with regular premiums paying for services when needed. Indeed, it is probable that fire insurance companies themselves would include the fire fighting services in their premiums, for insurance companies have a built-in interest in seeing to it that the fire damage suffered by their clients be as small as possible. On the other hand, those people who are capable of putting out their own fires or who have built their houses with specially fireproof material, may prefer not to pay for any fire fighting services. Residents of Hispanic-American neighborhoods may prefer to patronize Spanish-speaking fire companies. Each home-owner is permitted to choose and pay for any form of fire fighting that he prefers. In this way, the free market allows a maximum range of individual choice, while actual or potential competition keeps costs low and the quality of service high. And the private firemen, eager to please their customers, will scarcely stoop to the common arrogant practice of government firemen of wantonly destroying more of the fire victims' property, through ax and water, than might be lost in the fire itself. Private fire companies depend for their income on satisfied customers, while government fire departments mulct the hapless coerced taxpayer.

Similar solutions could be worked out for the supply of all services now performed by government. At one time or other in the past, all of these services were supplied in the free market; now of course they could be performed with the aid of modern technology.

Let's pause for a moment to consider the opposing view. Suppose that the advocates of taxation are right, that taxation is legitimate and moral, that the people are in some sense "voluntarily" paying taxes for services offered them by the government. In that case, *what criteria* can the pro-taxers offer for *how high* taxation should be and who should be taxed? The private market offers a variety of goods and services, each one of them desired by various members of the consuming public. And yet, we all know that there can be too much of a good thing: we don't put *all* our resources, all of our land, labor and capital, for example, into hi-fi sets, or bread, or bubble gum or concerts. For the more resources that go into these products, the *less* can go into the production of still other goods and services desired by consumers. There must be a balance between all these desired products. One of the glorious things about the free market is that it *itself* provides such a balance without coercion. If too much of one thing is produced and too little of another, costs become higher than prices in the first industry, businessmen suffer losses, and resources flow into those industries where profits can be made because not enough is being produced.

Thus the price system, and profit-and-loss signals on the free market, direct all resources in such a way as to supply efficiently for consumers the most desired goods and services.

But where are the criteria for taxation and for government services? The answer is that *there are none*, because taxes are extracted by coercion from the public. Those taxes are limitless, for there is no built-in balance to keep them in check. There is no profit-and-loss test for government activities, because the government can always cover its inefficiencies by taxing the public still more. And so, even if we believed that all government services were beneficial, there is no way to keep them in balance with private services; the tax level and who pays the taxes are purely arbitrary, necessarily decided not by economic criteria (for there are none) but by who controls the levers of political power. Taxes and government spending grow and feed upon themselves until the productive economy—and individual freedom—shrivel and die.

Thus, taxation is more than organized theft; it is an arbitrary system that leaves us at sea without a rudder. Apologists for statism have long led us to believe that freedom, while cherished by most of us, can only bring "chaos," while taxation and government action are needed to impose "order." In truth it is freedom and the free market that give us a balanced and harmonious economic order; it is government and taxation that bring chaos and arbitrary power.

The choice is quite clear. It is between freedom, prosperity and order on the one hand; taxation, tyranny, impoverishment and chaos on the other. Faced with the fundamental choice, we should see clearly that what we desperately need to do is not to limit or reform the tax system, but to abolish it.

QUESTIONS FOR DISCUSSION

1. Why is the title a good one?

2. How is the attention step developed?

3. What is the problem?

4. What is the solution?

5. What is accomplished in the last paragraph?

6. Discuss the effectiveness of the analogy of taxation and robbery.

7. The author, in developing the problem, makes the assertion that "There is no difference between taxation and robbery." Can you think of any differences?

8. The author, in developing his solution, makes the assertion that "The example of the post office can be extended to all of the other services provided and monopolized by the government." Can you think of services that might *not* be supplied more efficiently, cheaply, and morally by full competition?

9. In which ways would you agree or disagree with the author of this selection? Can you think of other problems related to government and/or taxation? What solutions would you propose?

10. For other examples of persuasive speeches, read the two speeches on capital punishment at the beginning of Part 4 of this text.

7

SUPPORTING ONE POINT

In social conversations and class discussions, at club meetings and even at parties, one often finds oneself in the position of having made an assertion that must now be explained, supported, and perhaps defended. On such occasions a knowledge of the kinds of material to use in developing your point can be of real value. The reason is not so much that being unable to explain and support your assertion is embarrassing as that it is uncommunicative. It's important that you share your convictions with people you talk to. Sharing them means fully developing them, so that people understand exactly what your belief is and what evidence led you to adopt it.

Experience in supporting one point will also be valuable to you because longer spoken and written communication generally consists of a series of points (main points and subordinate ones) tied together in a logical organizational pattern. If you can develop one point well, you can also develop a series of points. Supporting one point is a skill that is basic to longer and more complex communication experiences.

ASSIGNMENT

Think over some of the assertions you have made recently in discussions and conversations. You may have said that something was or was not true, was or was not good or right, should or should not have been done. You may have pointed out a major cause or effect, problem or solution, advantage or disadvantage of something. Select a point you feel strongly about and think your audience will (or should) feel strongly about too, and plan to talk to your class about it.

STATEMENT OF POINT

State your point in a simple declarative sentence. For example:

One of the gravest problems facing the world of the future is over-population.
The major cause of fires in the home is carelessness.
The phonics method is a very effective way to teach reading.
Turnstile justice is a folly that often allows crime to go unpunished.
Communist Party membership in the United States is declining.

PRELIMINARY DEVELOPMENT

Examine your assertion carefully and objectively. You will need to back it up with examples, with statistics and facts, with quotations by authorities. Write down the support you already have and the support you need to get, and begin doing research to fill out the development of your idea. Your research may, of course, be in written sources, but don't overlook the possibility of gathering your own facts through planned observation and interviews with knowledgeable people on your campus or in your community. Their testimony will have more immediacy for your audience than the opinion of a distant authority, and it may be equally valid.

Interviewing, observing, gathering your own facts, and making your own statistical summaries can be a very enjoyable and rewarding activity. For one thing, it brings you into contact with new and interesting people. For another, in gathering, selecting, and organizing your own material you will be doing original work that calls for considerable creativity.

In your research, gather more material than you can possibly use in your speech. Then select the details that will make your point most clearly and most dramatically. Be as specific as you can. For example, "light travels very fast" is a true statement but not an interesting one. "Scientists have computed the speed of light at approximately 186 thousand miles a second" is somewhat better. Better still would be to go one step further and show what the speed of light means in familiar terms: "To reach the sun, which is 93 million miles away, a traveler going at the standard highway speed of sixty miles an hour would take 10,600 years. Light travels the same distance in eight minutes!"

While you are doing your research, keep an open mind. You may want to change your opinion if the evidence on the other side is really more convincing or modify your position to take new information into account. When I was college student, in one of my classes we were to debate legalized prostitution. I volunteered to argue in favor of legalized prostitution because I really believed that legalization would be the best course. However, after I had done a good deal of reading on both sides of the question and interviewed several doctors, I changed my mind. It seemed to me that the arguments against it were stronger, more valid, and supported by more conclusive evidence.

ORGANIZATION

There are many ways to organize the material for supporting one point. The organization suggested below is one of the best because it is convincing to the audience; it is also a good one for you to learn at this stage because it will show you the kinds of material you can use and how to relate them to each other. In this assignment, follow it as closely as possible.

1. State your point clearly in the first sentence.

2. Use the explanatory techniques described below (definition, explanation, comparison, and restatement) to clarify and emphasize your point.

3. Use an illustration (anecdote) that will further clarify the point as you have explained it. At the same time, the anecdote should support the point by showing an actual case.

4. Use a series of instances (short, undeveloped examples given in a sentence or two) to support the illustration by showing that it is not an isolated case.

5. Use statistics or quotations for authority.

6. Restate your point for final emphasis.

FURTHER DEVELOPMENT

DEFINITION

Are there any words in your point as stated that might not be clear to your audience? If so, you will need to define them. Technical terms and unfamiliar words are obvious candidates, but remember that many common words need clarifying as well, because they can have more than one meaning. For example, if your point is that there is too much violence in TV westerns, you will need to explain what you mean by violence: killing of all sorts, or just when it seems out of proportion to the crime? What about fistfights? throwing bottles at barroom mirrors?

Define any word in your assertion that could possibly be misinterpreted or misunderstood by your audience. You may define a word by quoting a definition from the dictionary, a textbook, or a technical manual; you may define it in more personal terms by explaining what it

131

means to you; you may define it by listing what it includes and what it does not include, either in general or in the context of your speech.

EXPLANATION

Besides defining terms, you may need to explain your assertion. If your statement concerns an event (past, present, or future), explain how, when, where, why, and under what conditions. Be specific, and use as much detail as the audience needs to re-create the event in their own minds. You can give your own explanation if you wish, or quote from your research material, or use a combination of the two, depending on what the point is and how much you know about it. Visual aids can be very helpful in this part of your talk.

COMPARISON

Comparison is a specific technique that you may want to use to clarify your definitions and explanations. When you are talking about something outside the experience of your audience, compare it with something within their experience. You may compare it with something that it resembles in a literal way (you could compare another college with your own, another country with the United States, and so forth); or you may compare it to something that it resembles in a figurative way ("New York City is both the heart and the brain of the Northeast"; "Playing hard rock for my great aunt was like trying to feed raw meat to an African violet"). Careful and specific literal comparisons can help you prove a point as well as clarify it, but figurative comparisons are useful only to help your listeners see what you mean. Analogies, metaphors, and similes are often clear and vivid, but their purpose is to explain your point, not to provide evidence for it.

RESTATEMENT

Some points are straightforward enough not to require definition, explanation, or comparison, but you still need some kind of general explanatory material for emphasis. If you do not need to define, explain, or compare, simply make your point again in different words. Restatement will fix the point in the minds of your listeners, and repeating it in different words will ensure that the audience has understood you. Even if you have used other explanatory material, your may want to restate your point, rephrasing it or repeating your opening statement. Restatement is one of the best means of emphasizing an idea.

ILLUSTRATIONS AND INSTANCES

After you have used whatever general explanatory materials are needed, you should get down to specific cases. You need an illustration (anecdote) to clarify and support what you have said. In planning this, remember what you learned from your own experience and from observing others in Telling Your Experience to Make a Point (Chapter 3) and Speaking with Anecdotes (Chapter 6). Select and emphasize details in the anecdote that will develop your point, and use vivid descriptions, actions, and delivery patterns in order to get the emotional impact you want. The suspense and human interest in your story will be good attention-getters, and the emotional impact—if you plan it properly—can help persuade the audience to accept your assertion.

After your main illustration, you should mention three or four additional cases that also support your point. These should be very brief; a phrase or sentence for each is enough. Just identify the case by name or in some other specific way and show how it relates to your point.

Before you select specific instances, look over the explanatory section of your talk. Then try to produce an instance that will support each statement that needs support. This way you can support all your generalizations and avoid becoming too repetitious, as you might if you simply cited instances that back up your anecdote.

APPEALS TO AUTHORITY

As final support for your point, use statistics or a quotation from an authority. Up to this point, the audience has been largely taking your word for it. Facts that support your position and quotations by authorities who agree with you are particularly effective near the end of a talk, because that placement gives emphasis to the material. Appeals to authority are usually less effective at the beginning of a talk. Statistics and factual statements by experts tend to be very specific, and they may not lead smoothly to other developmental materials.

If you use statistics, give them in round numbers (one out of five, ninety-five percent, and so forth) so that the audience can grasp them easily. If you use a quotation, be sure to credit the source of the quotation and to mention briefly the person's credentials as an authority, perhaps as a transition to the quotation. Giving credit shows your honesty and your research, and mentioning the person's credentials shows the audience why they should pay attention to his or her opinion.

CONCLUSION

During the concluding part of the speech, restate your point. If possible, do this when you cite statistics or expert opinion. If the authority you quote says the same thing you said at the beginning, you can let him or her restate the point for you. If not, restate it yourself, to be sure that your audience has understood it and will remember it.

Read and analyze the sample manuscript at the end of this chapter. Then make two copies of the outline for your speech on the forms provided. Give one outline to your instructor, with the blank evaluation form provided for his or her use, and keep the other for your own use in practicing and delivering your talk.

PRACTICE

Study your summary of criticisms from the last assignment. As you practice your speech, begin working on the specific aspects of your presentation that need improvement.

DELIVERY

Some reminders:
1. Enter and exit firmly and confidently.
2. Maintain a friendly and enthusiastic manner.
3. Keep your voice firm and strong.
4. Emphasize important points with vocal inflections, gestures, and movement.
5. Complete all movements and gestures—don't let them be indefinite or weak.
6. Give your final line a strong delivery.
7. Maintain good eye contact throughout.
8. Use dialogue, gestures, and facial expressions to suggest the characters in your anecdotes.
9. If you plan to use visual aids to emphasize your points, prepare them carefully in advance and rehearse their use so that you can handle them with authority and confidence when you are delivering your speech.

For quoted material, you can bring the book or magazine along and read from it at the appropriate time, but practice the reading several times in advance so that you can look at the audience more than the book. Reading quotations from the source itself saves you time, prevents copying errors, and gives you something to do with your hands for at least part of the speech. More importantly, it gives the quotation more impact by making the audience feel a little closer to the source.

Books are not as easy to handle in front of a group as they look, so do some practicing beforehand. Decide where you will put the book before and after you use it, when and how you will pick it up, how you will hold it, and how you will return it to its place. Use a dependable bookmark (the best one I have found is a paper clip) so that you can't lose your place.

CRITICISM

This time focus your attention on the material used to develop the point each speaker is making. Which of the materials he or she used was most effective, and why? Where could improvement be made? Use the check list for developmental materials on your outline to assist you.

SAMPLE STUDENT MANUSCRIPT

(1) One of the advantages of driving a sports car is that it is easy to handle. By "easy to handle" I mean it operates well in heavy traffic, parks with little or no difficulty, and performs well on steep or winding roads.

(2) To illustrate my point of the ease in handling a sports car, I will relate some personal experiences. One day, while driving in the business district of San Jose, I had an unforgettable experience. Having moved to the San Jose area just two months before, I was unfamiliar with the pattern of one-way streets. As I entered downtown San Jose on First Street, I was busily engaged in a conversation with a friend who was riding with me. I had noticed that the street had two-way traffic when I turned off onto a side street, but I did not notice that First Street became a one-way street two blocks down. When I reentered First Street to return, I was about three blocks down from where I left. When I made the turn onto First Street, I noticed several cars racing towards me. I realized the situation and quickly turned the car around in the middle of the street and proceeded in the right direction. It was because I was driving a sports car that I was able to turn around in one, quick, easy operation.

(3) Another example of easy handling was when I took a trip into Redwoods State Park over a narrow, winding, mountain road. A few friends and I had decided to take a ride over into the park one weekend. There were three cars among us, including the sports car. The other two were late-model, full-size American makes, of over three hundred horsepower each. I led out as we started up the grade together. When I arrived at the park, sometime later, I was about twenty minutes ahead of the others because of the fine handling of the sports car around the curves.

(4) I have also had several good experiences with the ease in parking. On one occasion in particular, I had driven to keep an appointment in Redwood City and was looking for a parking space when I noticed one that two other cars had parked over into which would not leave enough room for an ordinary car. But because I had a small car, I was able to steer into the small space and thereby save much time and effort.

(5) In a special report written by the magazine *U.S. News and World Report* some owners of sports cars were asked to give their opinion on why they drove these cars. They said they like the "feel" of driving a sports car. They handle well, steer easily and take corners with more ease than the larger American cars. The driver has a feeling of greater control over his automobile and finds that it parks easier in less space, too. Some husbands report that after their wives have learned to operate the manual gearshift, they refuse to drive American cars even though they are equipped with additional accessories.

QUESTIONS FOR DISCUSSION

1. The first sentence in paragraph 1 states the point. The second sentence defines "easy to handle." Are any other definitions or explanations needed?

2. What is the purpose of the first sentence in paragraph 2? How could it be improved?

3. What weaknesses do you find in paragraph 2?

4. What additional information might be added in the last two sentences of paragraph 2 to emphasize the ease in handling?

5. Paragraph 3 gives some good, specific facts: late-model, full-sized American makes, over three hundred horsepower each, and twenty minutes ahead. What additional facts are needed to develop the comparison?

6. What additional facts might be added in paragraph 4 to emphasize the ease in parking?

7. The author of this selection has used his own experience exclusively. What are the advantages and disadvantages of doing this?

8. In his definition the author uses three phrases to define "easy to handle." Does he support each of the three phrases with an example?

OUTLINE: SUPPORTING ONE POINT

ASSERTION

GENERAL EXPLANATORY MATERIAL
(definition, explanation, comparison, restatement)

OUTLINE: SUPPORTING ONE POINT

ILLUSTRATION OR ANECDOTE

SUPPORTING INSTANCES

OUTLINE: SUPPORTING ONE POINT

STATISTICS AND/OR QUOTATIONS

RESTATEMENT

OUTLINE: SUPPORTING ONE POINT

BIBLIOGRAPHY

CHECK LIST FOR DEVELOPMENTAL MATERIALS

1. Do I have enough material to develop my point fully?
2. Is all my material relevant to my point?
3. Is my material suitable for my audience and my topic?
4. Are the sources of my material reliable?
5. Have I given appropriate credit to my sources?
6. Is my choice of words specific, vivid, and appropriate?

OUTLINE: SUPPORTING ONE POINT

ASSERTION

GENERAL EXPLANATORY MATERIAL
(definition, explanation, comparison, restatement)

OUTLINE: SUPPORTING ONE POINT

ILLUSTRATION OR ANECDOTE

SUPPORTING INSTANCES

OUTLINE: SUPPORTING ONE POINT

STATISTICS AND/OR QUOTATIONS

RESTATEMENT

OUTLINE: SUPPORTING ONE POINT

BIBLIOGRAPHY

CHECK LIST FOR DEVELOPMENTAL MATERIALS

1. Do I have enough material to develop my point fully?
2. Is all my material relevant to my point?
3. Is my material suitable for my audience and my topic?
4. Are the sources of my material reliable?
5. Have I given appropriate credit to my sources?
6. Is my choice of words specific, vivid, and appropriate?

INSTRUCTOR'S EVALUATION:

SUPPORTING ONE POINT

1 Delivery

A. Voice

B. Manner

C. Posture

D. Appearance

E. Gestures

F. Eye contact

G. Movement

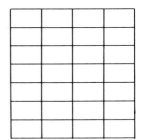

Excellent	Good	Fair	Poor

2 Material

A. Assertion

B. Definition

C. Explanation

D. Comparison

E. Restatement (preliminary)

F. Illustrations

G. Instances

H. Statistics

I. Quotations

J. Restatement (final)

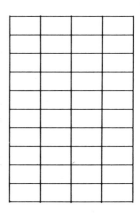

INSTRUCTOR'S EVALUATION:

SUPPORTING ONE POINT

	Excellent	Good	Fair	Poor
3 Language				
A. Vocabulary				
B. Sentence structure				

4 Comments

GRADE _____   INSTRUCTOR _____

8

TAKING A SIDE ON A CONTROVERSIAL ISSUE

It is difficult to know anything for sure. What is impossible today may be commonplace tomorrow; what is truth today may be proven fallacy tomorrow. What is considered good in one part of the world may be considered evil in another; an intelligent course of action in one situation may be disastrous under other circumstances.

Therefore controversy is continually developing over what is possible, what is true, what is good, what should be done. Just as smoke is a sign of fire, controversy is a sign that a problem exists. People who can see a problem, state it clearly, and offer intelligent, attractive solutions to it become leaders at home, at school, at work, and in the larger society as well. They are also better able to evaluate the positions others take on issues that concern them.

ASSIGNMENT

Examine your position on some controversial issues, especially issues on which there is an opposite position that someone else might hold. Try to define exactly what you believe and why you believe it. Think about possible alternatives and why other people might choose them. Plan to share one of your convictions with your audience, so that they can consider and perhaps adopt your view.

SUBJECT

Any will do. You may select an international problem such as war, NATO, or population control; a national problem such as taxes, law enforcement, or poverty; a campus problem such as cheating, required courses, or student power; a personal problem such as religion, sex, health, or standards of behavior. The important thing is that you select a real problem about which you have strong feelings. Remember, you are talking to real people and what you say may influence what they believe and what they do. So be sure you believe that what you propose is right, and that it is in the very best interests of your audience.

THESIS

State your position in a simple declarative sentence. Here are some examples:

We should increase foreign aid.
We should withdraw from the United Nations.
We should legalize gambling.
We should abolish the electoral system.
More students should participate in student government.
We should adopt the honor system to stop cheating on exams.
Laws on hallucinatory drugs should be liberalized.
College students should remain chaste until they are married.
We should adopt the pass-fail system of grading.
Students should take part in evaluating instructors.
The teachings of science are not incompatible with the teachings of religion.
Boxing should be abolished.
Capital punishment should be abolished.
We should adopt Esperanto as an international language.
Civil disobedience is the best way for minority groups to get our laws changed.
Smoking causes cancer.

Although you should choose an issue you feel strongly about, do not take an absolute yes-or-no stand if that would misrepresent what you believe. You can clarify your position by stating certain qualifications, conditions, or cases. For example, you may feel that abortion should be legal only in cases involving rape or incest.

ORGANIZATION

Your speech should be organized into five sections. Your first step is to get the attention of the audience. In the second section you describe the problem. In the third, you advocate a solution. In the fourth, you help the audience visualize the results of adopting your solution. In the final section, you call for action.

DEVELOPMENT

ATTENTION STEP

To get the attention of the audience, you can use a vivid illustration, a dramatic statement, a forceful question, a touch of humor, or a remark (perhaps complimentary) about the mood or interests of the audience.

DESCRIBING THE PROBLEM

In describing the problem, follow the suggestions given in Chapter 7 for developing one point. State the problem clearly and briefly. Define words where needed and explain how, when, where, and why the problem has developed. Show the impact of the problem on people by using vivid anecdotes and supporting instances. Use statistics and testimony to emphasize the size, scope, and importance of the problem. Make the problem real for the audience by explaining how it relates to their interests and needs; by showing the problem in familiar, concrete terms; by asking rhetorical questions, which will cause the audience to think even though they do not respond verbally; and by using striking facts.

PROPOSING A SOLUTION

When you present your solution, follow a procedure similar to the one you used in describing the problem. State the solution clearly and briefly. Define words where needed. Explain specifically how what you advocate will solve the problem as stated—and without creating new and greater problems. Remember what you decided when you were thinking about why other people might choose different alternatives, so that you can anticipate your listeners' objections and questions. Where you foresee resistance, don't play ostrich by sticking your head in the sand and hoping the objections will go away. Instead, acknowledge the objections yourself, directly or indirectly, and answer them in an open, friendly way.

Sometimes it may be possible to dispose of objections through satire or ridicule. These techniques can be very effective, although they are rhetorical devices rather than logical proofs. If you choose to use them, be careful not to ridicule specific members of the audience, for this could alienate the whole group and prevent an open-minded consideration of your position.

To support your solution, you must use logic. There are four kinds at your disposal: comparison, deduction, induction, and causal reasoning.

In *comparison* you reason that if something worked or failed in one situation it will work or fail in the one you are discussing. However, it is essential to show that the two situations are similar in important ways relating specifically to your problem and your solution.

In *deduction* you apply a general rule to a specific case. For example, urban renewal has been effective in cities throughout the country; therefore it will be effective in your city. For deduction to be convincing, you must prove with examples, statistics, and testimony that your generalization is true, and you must show that it really applies to the specific case you are discussing.

Induction (sometimes called the scientific method) involves reasoning from a series of specific instances to a general conclusion. For example, urban renewal was effective in A city, B city, C city, and D city; therefore urban renewal is effective in general. This kind of reasoning is used a great deal in public opinion polls and behavior studies as well as in scientific experiments. It can be especially persuasive if your examples are given in the form of anecdotes and instances supported by statistics. If your generalization has any outstanding exceptions, you would do well to mention the exceptions and show specifically how and why they are really exceptions and not the rule.

Causal reasoning deals with cause and effect. You either begin with an effect and reason back to the probable cause (juvenile delinquency has declined in our city because we have had a program of slum clearance), or you look at a cause and reason ahead to its probable effect (we are beginning a program of slum clearance, so we can expect a decline in juvenile delinquency). Reasoning from effect back to cause is important in understanding a problem and how it developed, since finding a solution to a problem is difficult unless you know its cause. Reasoning from cause to effect is important in presenting a solution, because a solution must be seen as the cause of a desirable future effect. No matter which direction your reasoning takes, be sure to show that a casual relationship does exist and that the cause is powerful enough to produce the effect.

VISUALIZING THE RESULTS

After you have presented your solution and the arguments in its favor, help the audience visualize the results your proposal would have. Show what will happen if your solution is adopted, what will happen if it is not adopted, or both. Use your imagination to project yourself and your audience into the future. Through vivid description and hypothetical examples, show them what it will be like, and support your projections with testimony by authorities.

CALLING FOR ACTION

Finally, call for action, in as practical and specific a way as possible. Think about who your listeners are and what interests and skills they have. Show them what they can do, individually and collectively, to put your plan into operation and achieve the results you have visualized. End on a positive, optimistic note that will make your listeners feel that they *can* and *will* do what you ask.

Before completing your outline, reread and analyze the article by Murray N. Rothbard that begins on page 119 and the sample student outline at the end of this chapter. Then make two copies of the outline for your speech, on the forms provided. In addition, use page 164 to analyze the kinds of logic and reasoning you are using. This analysis will help you evaluate your own logic objectively and make it easier for you to recognize and criticize the logic of others.

Hand in your Analysis of Logic, one copy of your outline, and the blank instructor's evaluation form. Keep the second copy of your outline for your own use in practicing and delivering your speech.

PRACTICE

Working with your outline, practice your speech aloud until you have achieved control of your material and polish in your delivery. Each time you practice, go through the whole speech without stopping, so that your presentation will have continuity and flow. If your memory fails here and there, ad lib. Then go back to the outline, study the places where you had trouble, and go through the whole speech again.

Practice part of the time alone, part of the time in front of a mirror, and part of the time before parents and friends. Get your parents and friends to offer suggestions for improvement in both your material and your delivery.

Remember to use your own words throughout, to be sure that your conclusions are based on your own thought and research, and to use your own experience wherever possible. Your listeners want to know that you have done careful research on your proposal, but they also want to feel that the ideas and the personality you are presenting are yours.

DELIVERY

Everything required for good delivery of any speech becomes even more important in a speech to persuade. You must maintain good eye contact throughout to communicate your sincerity; if you fail to look at your audience, they may suspect a lack of honesty on your part. Your movements, gestures, and voice must be firm and strong to indicate confidence in yourself and in your arguments; a speech of this kind puts you in a leadership position, and people will not follow someone who lacks self-confidence or confidence in his or her proposals. You must emphasize your important points with vocal inflections, gestures, and visual aids so your listeners can follow the logical steps in your argument. And you must use dialogue, gestures, and facial expressions throughout your speech, especially in your anecdotes, to convey your own feelings about the problem and to help the audience feel the emotional impact of the problem as well as understand it.

CRITICISM

Give particular attention this time to the logic others use in their speeches. Which uses of logic were particularly effective? How were they developed? Which logical arguments fell short? How could they have been improved? Use the check list for logic given at the end of your outline to assist you.

SAMPLE STUDENT OUTLINE

ATTENTION STEP

I Anecdote about a friend's request for abortion information from me.

II My friend bears out all that I have read regarding who has abortions: that the bulk of abortions are performed on married women as a means of birth control.

DESCRIPTION OF PROBLEM

I Because prohibitive laws have not prevented abortion, I feel that abortion should no longer be regulated by law. Rather, it should be the decision of a woman and her doctor alone, as with any other surgical procedure.

   A. Who gets abortions?

      1. Alice Rossi, in *Public Views on Abortion,* says that one in every two or three married women may undergo an illegal abortion during the years between thirty and fifty.

         a) In the United States over half the abortions are on married women.

            (1) Sherri Finkbine was married.

            (2) My friend was married.

            (3) An article from the *San Francisco Chronicle* of October 9 told of the death of a Mrs. Mooney from an abortion performed by a cocktail waitress. It went on to say Mrs. Mooney had four children.

      2. Dr. Garrett Hardin, in *Abortion and Human Dignity,* said, "In California any knowledgeable woman with five hundred dollars in her purse can secure an abortion."

         a) The forces opposing abortion, religious and moral, have *not* accomplished their stated goals of maintaining morality and preventing abortions.

         b) Dr. Alan F. Guttmacher says that we have about 800 thousand abortions a year.

         c) We have more than five thousand deaths a year from illegal abortions.

   B. Why do women seek abortions?

      1. Abortion is an after-the-fact birth control measure.

      a) I think it's a very sad solution, something I personally could never do.

      b) I'm afraid I would be one who would, if you'll pardon the pun, grin and bear it.

      c) Despite the crudity, induced abortion remains for most of the world the surest method of family regulation available.

      d) It is not a dangerous operation if done in the first three months of pregnancy. Childbirth is four times as dangerous.

C. On November 8, 1967, the California Therapeutic Abortion Act became effective. You may wonder who will benefit from this change.

    1. Before Reagan emasculated the Act, Bielenson, the author of the bill, stated that his Act would benefit only two to five percent of the women undergoing illegal abortions in California.

    2. The mechanics of the law itself are such that delays are inevitable. A decision is forestalled until the woman is past the twentieth week, by which time nothing can be done. The risk of death goes from six in 100 thousand if abortion is done in the first three months to three hundred in 100 thousand if done later.

    3. Therapeutic abortions may only be performed in hospitals larger than twenty-five beds. This excludes 131 of California's 565 licensed hospitals, which certainly seems to me to be discrimination.

    4. If German measles is contracted within the first trimester of pregnancy, there is a fifty-fifty chance that the woman will have a deformed child. However, women desiring to abort potentially deformed babies cannot get a legal abortion in California.

    5. Where will these women who are turned down by our new law go for the abortion which they feel they must have?

II I have stressed that most abortions are performed on married women, but that does not mean that they are the only group seeking abortions.

A. Many young teenage girls unfortunately find themselves with the problem of an unwanted pregnancy.

    1. There seem to be only a few choices, all bad, open to a girl in this situation.

      a) She can marry, and be one of the eighty-five percent of

teenage brides who is already pregnant. According to Dan Lion, minister at the Palo Alto Unitarian Church, fifty percent of these marriages end in divorce.

b) She can go to a home for unwed mothers.

c) Or she can be one of the seventy percent of pregnant single girls who turn to abortion rather than marry or bear an illegitimate child.

B. Is it good for a woman, teenage or older, to bear a child she truly doesn't want?

1. An unwanted child is a social danger.

a) According to Dr. Hardin, unwanted children are more likely to become delinquents and to be poor parents themselves, breeding another generation of unwanted children.

b) We can force a woman to have a child but not to want one.

PROPOSED SOLUTION

I   I feel strongly that we must continue to work to erase laws on abortion from the statute books and make abortion the woman's own decision and that of her own doctor.

A. I hope you all understand I am *not* urging abortion, but rather the freedom to choose it as a means of birth control if one must. Foolproof birth control, and information on birth control, is what is needed so that abortion can become a thing of the past.

B. What would relaxing or abolishing our abortion laws mean?

1. It would in no way infringe on the privileges of any group to hold its own definitions of moral and immoral behavior.

2. It would uphold the personal rights and human dignity of those who do *not* consider abortion immoral.

3. There is no other branch of medicine in which the legislature tries to prescribe what is good for the patient or which penalizes doctors for doing what they feel is in the patient's best interest.

4. It seems illogical to me that in today's overcrowded world the woman who wishes to avoid having an unwanted child is punished and the woman with a big family is praised and admired.

C. More liberal or no laws have worked in erasing the bulk of deaths from illegal abortions in Japan, the Soviet Union, and Puerto Rico.

D. What are the objections to removing these laws from our statute books?

    1. The Catholic Church considers abortion as going against the sixth Commandment, "Thou shalt not kill."

        a) However, we do permit legal killings in self-defense and in war, and the state kills certain convicted criminals to protect innocent people or society, and the Church remains silent.

        b) As Herb Caen put it, "When they have funerals for miscarriages, I'll believe abortion is murder."

    2. The other big objection seems to be that legalized abortion will increase promiscuity.

        a) I suppose this is a possibility, but again I repeat that the bulk of abortions are done on married women.

        b) This is also the objection raised against the birth control pill.

        c) Some people will always be promiscuous, just as some people will always speed whether or not there are laws against speeding.

VISUALIZATION OF RESULTS

I If the laws are abolished or greatly liberalized:

    A. Every child will be a wanted child.

    B. Abortion will be controlled for quality, like any other surgical procedure.

    C. The underworld of abortionists for profit will crumble.

II If these archaic laws remain the law of the land:

    A. There will be more forced marriages, fifty percent of which will end in divorce.

    B. Abortions will continue to be dispensed according to ability to pay, and a woman will get the kind of abortion she can pay for.

    C. Open violation of the law will continue. There is one death from bungled abortion every hour in the United States.

APPEAL FOR ACTION

I Abortion should be a woman's own decision, based on a set of moral and religious values which is her own, and which only she can judge.

II   Since laws regulating abortion have failed to be effective, I feel the laws should be removed.

BIBLIOGRAPHY

San Jose Mercury, November 15, 1967, and November 6, 1967.

San Francisco Chronicle, October 9, 1967, and November 22, 1967.

Time, October 13, 1967.

Sherri Finkbine, *The Case for Legalized Abortion Now.* Berkeley, California: Diablo Press, 1967.

Alice S. Rossi

Marya Mannes

Dr. Lucile Newman

Dr. Garrett Hardin

Rev. F. Danford Lion

Harriet Pilpel

Dr. Jerome M. Kummer

Dr. Leslie Corsa, Jr.

Patricia Maginnis

Herbert Packer

Ralph J. Gampell

Dr. Christopher Tietze

QUESTIONS FOR DISCUSSION

1. If the opening anecdote is properly developed, what can be accomplished?

2. How does the speaker emphasize the size and importance of the problem?

3. What kinds of logic are used in describing the problem?

4. What kind of logic is emphasized in the proposed solution?

5. What two methods of development are used in the visualization of results?

6. What action is requested? Is the request a practical one?

7. Is the information in the bibliography complete? Is it given in proper form?

8. What objections to her solution does the speaker anticipate? What method does she use to answer the objections?

OUTLINE: TAKING A SIDE ON A CONTROVERSIAL ISSUE

ATTENTION STEP

DESCRIPTION OF PROBLEM

OUTLINE: TAKING A SIDE ON A CONTROVERSIAL ISSUE

PROPOSED SOLUTION

OUTLINE: TAKING A SIDE ON A CONTROVERSIAL ISSUE

VISUALIZATION OF RESULTS

OUTLINE: TAKING A SIDE ON A CONTROVERSIAL ISSUE

APPEAL FOR ACTION

OUTLINE: TAKING A SIDE ON A CONTROVERSIAL ISSUE

BIBLIOGRAPHY

OUTLINE: TAKING A SIDE ON A CONTROVERSIAL ISSUE

CHECK LIST FOR LOGIC

1. In comparisons, have I shown clearly and specifically that the two items are similar in important ways?
2. In deduction, have I proved that the generalization is true and that it applies to the situation I am discussing?
3. In induction, have I used enough examples? Have I explained any exceptions to my generalization?
4. In causal reasoning, have I shown that a causal relationship really exists and that the cause is strong enough to produce the effect?

NOTES:

OUTLINE: TAKING A SIDE ON A CONTROVERSIAL ISSUE

ATTENTION STEP

DESCRIPTION OF PROBLEM

OUTLINE: TAKING A SIDE ON A CONTROVERSIAL ISSUE

PROPOSED SOLUTION

OUTLINE: TAKING A SIDE ON A CONTROVERSIAL ISSUE

VISUALIZATION OF RESULTS

OUTLINE: TAKING A SIDE ON A CONTROVERSIAL ISSUE

APPEAL FOR ACTION

OUTLINE: TAKING A SIDE ON A CONTROVERSIAL ISSUE

BIBLIOGRAPHY

OUTLINE: TAKING A SIDE ON A CONTROVERSIAL ISSUE

CHECK LIST FOR LOGIC

1. In comparisons, have I shown clearly and specifically that the two items are similar in important ways?
2. In deduction, have I proved that the generalization is true and that it applies to the situation I am discussing?
3. In induction, have I used enough examples? Have I explained any exceptions to my generalization?
4. In causal reasoning, have I shown that a causal relationship really exists and that the cause is strong enough to produce the effect?

NOTES:

ANALYSIS OF LOGIC:

TAKING A SIDE ON A CONTROVERSIAL ISSUE

Which of the following have you used in your speech? Where and how have you used them? Be specific.

Comparison (comparing one item with another)

Deduction (applying a generalization to a specific case)

171

ANALYSIS OF LOGIC:

TAKING A SIDE ON A CONTROVERSIAL ISSUE

Induction (going from a series of examples to a general conclusion)

Causal reasoning (reasoning from effect to cause or from cause to effect)

INSTRUCTOR'S EVALUATION:

TAKING A SIDE ON A CONTROVERSIAL ISSUE

	Excellent	Good	Fair	Poor

1 Delivery

   A. Voice

   B. Manner

   C. Posture

   D. Appearance

   E. Gestures

   F. Eye contact

   G. Movement

2 Material

   A. Attention step

   B. Description of problem

   C. Proposed solution

   D. Visualization of results

   E. Appeal for action

3 Language

   A. Vocabulary

   B. Sentence structure

173

INSTRUCTOR'S EVALUATION:

TAKING A SIDE ON A CONTROVERSIAL ISSUE

4 Use of logic

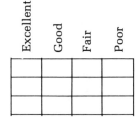

	Excellent	Good	Fair	Poor
A. Amount				
B. Clarity				
C. Emphasis				

5 Comments

GRADE _____ INSTRUCTOR _____

9
CALLING FOR ACTION

Members of a society belong to several kinds of groups: family groups, social groups, service organizations, professional organizations, and so on. The structure of these groups may be informal or formal, and the activities they engage in range from social conversation to highly organized political work. No one is the leader of all the groups he or she belongs to, but no one is always a follower either. Each person is at times a follower and at other times a leader.

Sometimes a person seeks the role of leader out of a sense of responsibility or a desire for status; sometimes a person is offered the role because he or she has leadership qualifications that the group recognizes. No matter how the leader gets the position, his or her responsibility is to get the group moving together toward its goals. To do this, he or she must be able to speak clearly and communicate directly, make suggestions in an attractive manner, and motivate the group to action.

ASSIGNMENT

Take a leadership role in your class. Examine your convictions about what you think members of the class should do for their own benefit as individuals, or for the benefit of the class, the college, or society at large. Choose an issue you feel strongly about. Decide specifically what you think the members of the class should do in relation to the issue and why you feel this way. What in your experience or knowledge convinces you that they should adopt this course of action?

Plan to present your suggestion to your listeners for their considera-tion. Be sure you have their best interests at heart, and show them in your material and your manner of presentation that you do.

SUBJECT

Any subject will do, but keep in mind that your primary goal is to get action in relation to that subject. As in the last assignment, you may select a controversial subject that has international, national, campus, or per-sonal importance. Or, if you prefer, you may select a subject that is not controversial but relates to the health, safety, welfare, or happiness of the members of your group.

THESIS

If you wish to speak on a controversial subject, look over the topics suggested in Chapter 8 and think through the topics covered by the members of your class in the last round of speeches. If you disagree with any of the positions stated, here is your chance to present the other side. For example, if someone argued that drug laws should be liberalized and you feel that drug laws should be kept as they are or tightened, take this opportunity to develop and present your arguments. If you'd rather speak on something less controversial this time, consider such topics as: you should take up jogging; you should install a fire alarm system in your home; you should invest your money in stocks while you're young; you should give of yourself to others. Now state your purpose in a sentence that makes clear what you want your group to do.

ORGANIZATION

As in the last assignment, your speech should be organized in five steps: (1) get attention, (2) describe the problem, (3) advocate a solution, (4) visualize the results, (5) call for action.

DEVELOPMENT

Follow all the suggestions given in your last assignment for develop-ing the five steps, giving special emphasis to the visualization and action steps. Once again, use logic and reason supported by examples, facts, statistics, and testimony to show your audience logically and reasonably what they should do.

In addition, work on the needs, desires, emotions, motives, and drives of your listeners. They should *want* to do what you recommend.

We all have an intellectual nature and an emotional nature. Frequently, our problems are a result of a conflict between the two. We know intellectually what we *should* do, but emotionally we want to do something else. Sometimes we are so torn by the conflict that we can't do anything. So if you want to be persuasive, you need to show your audience logically what they should do and work on their drives and motives to make them want to do it. Select emotional appeals with integrity, keeping the best interests of your audience in mind. Ask yourself what those interests are, and use them with honesty and sincerity in your speech.

Love, hate, fear, anger, sympathy, pride, jealousy, and affection are emotions that all people experience, but if you use any of them, develop them subtly. In pure form an appeal to the emotions can be too obvious to be effective; on the other hand, the emotions it arouses can be too strong to be controlled. In addition, hate, pride, and jealousy are often considered "base emotions," and you might be thought crude or immoral for appealing to them. Such appeals are often used effectively by demogogues, of course, and the intelligent person must be careful not to be taken in by them.

Motives are related to emotions, but they are more specific and easier to handle. Some common motives are: to make money; to compete successfully; to help others; to be healthy; to enjoy physical comforts; to have and raise children; to have friends; to have a clear conscience; to satisfy curiosity; to realize ideals; to have a worthwhile religion; to avoid danger; to be attractive to the opposite sex; to have freedom; to conform to customs; to gain approval; and to maintain self-respect.

You can develop these emotions and drives in your audience by sincerely stating your own feelings, by asking questions that will make your listeners recognize their own motives, by reading passages by writers who have expressed an emotion well, and especially by telling anecdotes. An anecdote can have a subtle but highly effective emotional impact. Its basic purpose is to serve as an example that clarifies and supports your position logically. When told well, with a wealth of specific detail, it also creates empathy for the central character. Members of the audience put themselves in the character's place, and they share the character's emotions and motives vicariously. Thus they can "feel" the problem as well as understand it, and you are working on both their logical and their emotional natures at the same time.

In the formation of every sentence, the selection of every detail and every word, remember that you must project your sincerity, honesty, integrity, and confidence to the audience. As sales people say, before you can sell your product, you must sell yourself. People are more likely to accept something from you—a product, an idea, a plan of action—if they respect and admire you.

In order to sell yourself, the first thing you need to indicate is that you know what you're talking about. You can do this in several ways: through anecdotes that show you have personal experience with your topic; through references to research sources that show you have studied the

177

problem carefully; and through your controlled, fluent, confident manner. In addition, you need to indicate sincerity, honesty, and integrity through statements showing that your motives are based on the best interests of your listeners, through details in your personal anecdotes that reveal those qualities in you (handle these details subtly and modestly for best results), and through a warm, friendly, sincere speaking manner and good eye contact. You cannot fake sincerity. Be sure you really feel it, and then simply allow it to come to the surface when you talk. Take every honest opportunity to make your audience feel important. You will make it easier for them to accept you and your ideas.

If some of those in your audience oppose your position your suggestions will be more attractive to them if you are indirect in your criticism of their position. Point out what is good or valid in it, and then point out how your suggestion will be an improvement. Don't say (or imply), "You're wrong"; instead say, "You're right as far as you go, but there are other aspects to be considered" (or something similar). This suggests an open mind on your part and encourages your listeners to have a similarly open-minded attitude. Be careful in your choice of pronouns. When giving compliments use *you* if possible ("You did this well."); and when pointing out problems, use *we* ("We have failed to do this.").

At this point, you should read and analyze the sample outline at the end of this chapter. Then make two copies of the outline for your speech, one for your own use and one for your instructor. In addition, make an analysis of the logic, the appeals to emotions and motives, and the methods of selling yourself that you plan to use. Forms are provided on pages 197–200; they should be turned in to your instructor with his or her copy of the outline and the blank instructor's evaluation sheet.

PRACTICE

Follow the suggestions for practicing given in Chapter 8, paying special attention throughout to naturalness and sincerity. It is important that you practice enough to gain absolute control of yourself, your material, and your language. Your delivery must not sound mechanical and memorized, however. Don't allow yourself to fall into emotionless repetitions of the words. Each time you go through your speech, re-create your original and honest feelings about your topic and your audience.

DELIVERY

Follow the suggestions given for delivery in Chapter 8. When delivering the anecdotes in your speech, remember what you learned from your own experience and by observing others in Chapter 2, Communicating Your Experience for Enjoyment. A little humorous exaggeration will help you get laughs where you want them; a more subtle style coupled with much specific detail will help you develop the deeper emotions. Above all, project your own honest feelings to your audience. Try not to think about yourself (do I look all right? do I sound all right? and so on). Instead, concentrate all your energy on your topic and your audience. Look at the audience, and adapt your delivery to their response. If they seem unconcerned, increase your energy and enthusiasm. If they seem overwhelmed, use more subtlety. Show that you consider them equal partners in the communication process and that you are eager to share this material with them because you sincerely believe it will be of real value to them.

CRITICISM

Give particular attention this time to the motivational and emotional appeals used by other speakers. Which were particularly effective? How were they developed? Which could have been effectively developed and were not? How could the development have been accomplished more effectively? Use the check list for persuasion at the end of your outline to assist you.

SAMPLE STUDENT OUTLINE

Subject: Physical fitness

Specific purpose: To make each member of the audience realize the vital importance of his or her individual responsibility for being physically fit and to persuade the audience to do their share in keeping physically fit.

ATTENTION STEP

I *Visual aid: D.O.A. stamp on the blackboard.* Have you ever seen this stamp before? Do you know what it means? D.O.A. . . . Dead on Arrival. This stamp is being put on more and more certificates of heart attack victims. Many people die from heart attacks because they are not physically fit. Fitness is a result of physical conditioning.

II Read two lines from sample death certificate.

III *Restatement.* Every day people are dying from heart attacks because they are not physically fit. The man I just read about had no previous heart condition. He just was not physically fit. He passed his margin of safety and reached the fatal attack.

DESCRIPTION OF PROBLEM

I In our growing nation of automation there is a vital need for Americans to take individual responsibility for physical fitness.

    A. Fitness is needed to better tolerate stresses. *Definition of "stress."* Stress can take such forms as a germ entering the body, work worries, death of a loved one, and countless others. Most forms of stress are essential and are harmful only to the unfit.

    B. Fitness gives one a sense of well-being.

        1. *Confidence:* Dr. Paul Dudley White said in his book *Fitness for the Whole Family* that a simple exercise program gives confidence and brings out true abilities and personality.

        2. *Endurance:* a physically fit person is capable of taking more strain and punishment than one who is not fit. John Walsh, in *The First Book on Physical Fitness,* gave a good illustration to this effect.

            a) *Illustration.* Bail-out of Colonel William Rankin. Colonel Rankin was flying at a height of fifty thousand feet when he was forced to bail out. He was improperly dressed and he bailed out into a violent thunderstorm. He tossed around for a half-hour in subfreezing temperatures, but he survived because of his superb physical condition.

b) *Specific instance.* Diane's medical operation. My friend Diane had a major operation. She recovered in a few weeks from an operation that usually requires several months because she was physically fit. She had enjoyed good exercise by playing tennis.

c) *Specific instance.* Dolores' medical operation. My friend Dolores had a major operation. She thought she would recover and go back to school in three weeks but it took one year. Dolores, unlike Diane, was not physically fit.

d) *Generalization.* As you can see from the operations of the two girls, physical fitness speeds recovery. It speeds it drastically. The girl who was not physically fit became anemic and required additional medical aid.

C. Physical fitness will increase chances of survival.

1. *Increase life span:* strong heart. According to the RCAF book on physical fitness, you may increase your life span by engaging in a program of fitness. A physically fit person has a stronger and more efficient heart.

2. *Balanced life:* helps increase life span. According to Dr. Hoffman in his book *Heart,* Americans must develop a balance between work and play. He says that Americans do not get enough physical activity, and when they get activity they often get too much at one time. This can often lead to a shortened life. This would not happen to a physically fit person.

II *Pointing statement* (relating to audience). Most of you in this classroom probably think that physical fitness is the concern of someone else. You may feel that you are too young or too healthy. Remember, you won't always be young, and you can be healthy and still not be physically fit. Your body, like anything else, must be cared for, and now is the time to begin a program of physical fitness before it is too late.

III *Summary statement.* You can see from the information I have given you that in this modern age there is a definite need for each individual to assume responsibility for physical fitness. Physical fitness increases chances of survival, helps one to better tolerate stresses, and helps one to enjoy life to its fullest extent.

PROPOSED SOLUTION

I The principles which help you to attain physical fitness are: proper diet, proper exercise, adequate sleep, and fresh air and sunshine or a written exercise plan.

A. Proper nutrition: first fundamental for fitness. Each individual should maintain a balanced diet to insure the growth of the body. *Statistics.* Overweight male. Dr. Robert Peale, a New York specialist in weight control, says statistics show that the average adult male is from ten to twenty pounds overweight.

B. Proper exercise: second fundamental for fitness. Exercise aids respiration, circulation, digestion, and elimination of body wastes. Our bodies cannot be strong and function properly without proper exercise.

C. Adequate sleep: third fundamental for fitness. Each individual requires a different amount of sleep. He must have a minimum amount of sleep in order to perform properly.

D. Fresh air and sunshine: fourth fundamental for fitness. The average adult does not naturally get all the fresh air he needs, so he must plan his time so that he does. This helps provide our body energy.

E. Written plans on physical fitness. There are many available written plans. Two good ones are the YMCA plan and the RCAF plan.

F. *Theoretical demonstration.* If you follow a regular exercise plan, it stands to reason that you will reap a good harvest. Like plants and wild animals, when people are cared for they will grow.

G. *Reference to a practical experience.* As I mentioned earlier, Colonel Rankin had a superb physical condition and it helped him survive. Dr. Paul Dudley White says that everyone should consider doing something about physical fitness, aside from those who are not able.

H. *Objections.* Some people may say they are too old, or too young, but it is never too late to begin a program of fitness.

II *Summary statement.* If you get a balanced diet, proper exercise, adequate fresh air and sunshine, and the proper sleep, you will have improved physical fitness.

VISUALIZATION OF RESULTS

I *Statement of negative projection.* If you just choose to sit back and not engage in a program of physical fitness, you will become soft and you will limit your body's resistance to fight off disease and worry. You may decrease your life span and become unhappy and irritable.

II *Statement of positive projection.* If you choose to begin a program of physical fitness, you will become stronger and will help your body to ward off disease and worry. You will have a healthy, happy outlook on life, look and be cheerful, and increase your chances for living to a ripe old age.

APPEAL FOR ACTION

I Everyone is talking about fitness—let's do something about it. Ten minutes each day can lead you on your way. Within one month, you will see a noticeable difference. Former President John F. Kennedy referred to physical fitness as one of our most valuable resources that should be preserved.

II *Restatement.* Physical fitness is the responsibility of each person. We do not want to become a generation of spectators, but we want to be participants. All of us must consider our own responsibilities in fitness and we will keep our country fit.

BIBLIOGRAPHY

Roger Duhamel, *Exercise Plans for Fitness*. Ottawa, Canada: Queen's Printer, 1966.

Harold Friermood, *The YMCA Guide to Adult Fitness*. New York: Association Press, Inc., 1963.

Rudolph Hoffman, *Heart*. New York: Doubleday & Company, Inc., 1962.

J. E. Walsh, *The First Book of Physical Fitness*. New York: Franklin Watts, Inc., 1964.

Paul Dudley White, *Fitness for the Whole Family*. New York: Doubleday & Company, Inc., 1964.

QUESTIONS FOR DISCUSSION

1. What emotion is developed in the attention step? Is it effective?

2. The basic motive appealed to is, of course, the desire to be healthy. What other motives are developed in the speech? Where? How? Are they suitable to the topic and to an audience like yours? Can you think of others that might be used?

3. Where has the speaker referred to her own experience? Why is this effective?

4. Are there other ways the speaker could (or should) use personal experience?

5. The problem is described largely through examples and testimony. Are statistics needed as well?

6. The solution recommends proper diet, proper exercise, adequate sleep, and fresh air and sunshine, but the speaker does not recommend specific plans for each. Why do you suppose she did not? Would the speech be more effective if she had?

7. Do the two parts of the visualization of results give enough specific material for both clarity and emotional impact?

8. Does the appeal for action offer specific suggestions on how to put her solution into operation?

9. The logic used in the speech is mostly cause and effect. How is it developed?

10. The pointing statement (Description of Problem, II) uses the pronoun *you* throughout. Might it be better to say *we*? Why or why not?

OUTLINE: CALLING FOR ACTION

ATTENTION STEP

DESCRIPTION OF PROBLEM

OUTLINE: CALLING FOR ACTION

PROPOSED SOLUTION

OUTLINE: CALLING FOR ACTION

VISUALIZATION OF RESULTS

OUTLINE: CALLING FOR ACTION

APPEAL FOR ACTION

OUTLINE: CALLING FOR ACTION

BIBLIOGRAPHY

OUTLINE: CALLING FOR ACTION

CHECK LIST FOR PERSUASION

1. Have I used personal experience to indicate my knowledge of the subject?
2. Have I credited my sources to show my honesty and my research?
3. Have I shown my sincerity, honesty, and integrity in direct statements, anecdotes, and delivery style?
4. Have I shown the audience that what I recommend is in their best interests?
5. In describing the problem, my solution, and its results, have I used enough specific detail in descriptions and anecdotes to make the audience feel the problem as well as understand it?
6. Have I told them in the appeal for action specifically how they can put my plan into operation?

NOTES:

OUTLINE: CALLING FOR ACTION

ATTENTION STEP

DESCRIPTION OF PROBLEM

OUTLINE: CALLING FOR ACTION

PROPOSED SOLUTION

OUTLINE: CALLING FOR ACTION

VISUALIZATION OF RESULTS

OUTLINE: CALLING FOR ACTION

APPEAL FOR ACTION

OUTLINE: CALLING FOR ACTION

BIBLIOGRAPHY

OUTLINE: CALLING FOR ACTION

CHECK LIST FOR PERSUASION

1. Have I used personal experience to indicate my knowledge of the subject?
2. Have I credited my sources to show my honesty and my research?
3. Have I shown my sincerity, honesty, and integrity in direct statements, anecdotes, and delivery style?
4. Have I shown the audience that what I recommend is in their best interests?
5. In describing the problem, my solution, and its results, have I used enough specific detail in descriptions and anecdotes to make the audience feel the problem as well as understand it?
6. Have I told them in the appeal for action specifically how they can put my plan into operation?

NOTES:

ANALYSIS OF LOGIC: CALLING FOR ACTION

Which of the following have you used in your speech? Where and how have you used them? Be specific.

Comparison (comparing one item to another)

Deduction (applying a generalization to a specific case)

ANALYSIS OF LOGIC: CALLING FOR ACTION

Induction (going from a series of examples to a general conclusion)

Causal reasoning (reasoning from effect to cause or from cause to effect)

ANALYSIS OF APPEALS TO EMOTIONS AND MOTIVES: CALLING FOR ACTION

Which emotions and motives will you appeal to in your speech? How and where (be specific)?

Emotions (refer to examples on page 177)

Motives (refer to examples on page 177)

ANALYSIS OF METHODS OF SELLING YOURSELF:
CALLING FOR ACTION

How will you do the following in your speech? Be specific about where and how.

Indicate your knowledge

Show your sincerity, honesty, integrity, good will, confidence

INSTRUCTOR'S EVALUATION:

CALLING FOR ACTION

	Excellent	Good	Fair	Poor

1 Delivery

    A. Voice

    B. Manner

    C. Posture

    D. Appearance

    E. Gestures

    F. Eye contact

    G. Movement

2 Material

    A. Attention step

    B. Description of problem

    C. Proposed solution

    D. Visualization of results

    E. Appeal for action

3 Language

    A. Vocabulary

    B. Sentence structure

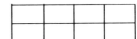

4 Use of logic

    A. Amount

    B. Clarity

    C. Emphasis

INSTRUCTOR'S EVALUATION:

CALLING FOR ACTION

	Excellent	Good	Fair	Poor
5 Use of emotions and motives				
A. Amount				
B. Development				
C. Suitability for audience				
D. Suitability for topic				

	Excellent	Good	Fair	Poor
6 Projecting favorable image				
A. Knowledge of subject				
B. Sincerity, honesty, integrity, and so forth				

7 Comments

GRADE _____   INSTRUCTOR _____

4
COMMUNICATING TO SOLVE PROBLEMS

Because effective communication is a pleasure, people are sometimes misled into thinking it is a luxury—enjoyable, but not essential. As a basic tool for solving problems, however, communication is a necessity of life. Undefined, unresolved problems eat away beneath the surface of an individual personality, and they can also undermine all group activities, from a casual conversation between two friends to formal negotiations between international powers.

The purpose of group discussion is the cooperative solution of problems. It requires people to bring the problems that concern them out into the open and to define them. Sometimes the clear definition of a problem is enough to make its solution evident. If not, the give-and-take of discussion makes it possible to consider intelligently all reasonable solutions and to select the one that seems best.

For this reason, problems in organizations and businesses are often solved by the group processes. It used to be believed that the best leader was one who could make decisions himself or herself and command and dictate on the basis of these decisions. In recent years leadership styles have changed, and it is now generally believed that the best leaders are those who can use the democratic processes of group discussion and decision making.

The assignments in Part 4 ask you to locate and define problems and actively to seek solutions for them in cooperation with others. If you take part honestly and openly, remembering to communicate yourself, the experience will add meaning to your personal relationships. It will also increase your understanding of the problems you share with other people, offer solutions to some of them, and suggest improved methods for finding solutions to the rest.

CAPITAL PUNISHMENT: DO WE REALLY NEED TO KILL PEOPLE TO TEACH PEOPLE THAT KILLING PEOPLE IS WRONG?

ANTHONY G. AMSTERDAM

> The two speeches on capital punishment reprinted here do not
> constitute a real group discussion, since the two men were not present at
> the same time to deliver them. However, the selections combined dem-
> onstrate many of the principles of group discussion to solve problems.
> Read the selections through once now. Later on, you will be asked to
> reread and analyze them, using the discussion questions that follow the
> second speech.

My discussion of capital punishment this afternoon will
proceed in three stages. *First,* I would like to set forth certain
basic factual realities about capital punishment, like the fact
that capital punishment is a fancy word for legally killing
people. Please forgive me for beginning with such obvious and
ugly facts. Much of our political and philosophical debate
about the death penalty is carried on in language calculated to
conceal these realities and their implications. The implications, I will suggest, are that capital punishment is a great evil:
surely the greatest evil except for war that our society can in-
tentionally choose to commit.

This does not mean that we should do away with capital
punishment. Some evils, like war, are occasionally necessary;
and perhaps capital punishment is one of them. But the fact
that it is a great evil means that we should not choose to do it
without some very good and solid reason of which we are
satisfactorily convinced upon sufficient evidence. The conclusion of my first point simply is that the burden of proof upon
the question of capital punishment rightly rests on those who
are asking us to use our laws to kill people with; and that this is
a very heavy burden.

Second, I want to review the justifications that have been
advanced to support capital punishment. I want to explore with

"Capital Punishment" by Anthony G. Amsterdam. From *Vital Speeches of the Day,* vol. 43, no. 22, Sept. 1,
1977. Reprinted by permission of the publisher, City News Publishing Co., Southold, N.Y.

you concepts such as retribution and deterrence, and some of the assumptions and evidence about them. The conclusion of my second point will be that none of the reasons which we like to give ourselves for executing criminals can begin to sustain the burden of proof that rightfully rests upon them.

Third, I would like to say a word about history—about the slow but absolutely certain progress of maturing civilization that will bring an inevitable end to the punishment of death. That history does not give us the choice between perpetuating and abolishing capital punishment, because we could not perpetuate it if we wanted to. Our choice is narrower but not unimportant: whether we shall be numbered among the last generations of legal killers, or remembered as the first generation to put legal killing aside. I will end by asking you to cast your choice for life instead of death. But, first, let me begin with some basic facts about the death penalty.

The most basic fact, of course, is that capital punishment means taking living, breathing men and women, stuffing them into a chair, strapping them down, pulling a lever, and exterminating them. We have almost forgotten this fact because there have been no executions in this country for more than ten years, except for Gary Gilmore whose combined suicide and circus were so wildly extravagant as to seem unreal. For many people, capital punishment has become a sanitized and symbolic issue: Do you or do you not support your local police? Do you or do you not care enough about crime to get tough with criminals? These abstractions were never what capital punishment was about, although it was possible to think so during the ten-year moratorium on executions caused by consitutional challenges to the death penalty in the courts. That is no longer possible. The courts have now said that we can start up executions again, if we want to. Today, a vote for capital punishment is a vote to kill real, live people.

What this means is, first, that we bring a man or woman into court and put them through a trial for their lives. They are expected to sit back quietly and observe decent courtroom decorum throughout a proceeding whose purpose is slowly and systematically to kill them. The jury hears evidence and votes; and you can always tell when a jury has voted for death because they come back into court and they will not look the defendant or defense counsel in the eyes. The judge pronounces sentence and the defendant is taken away to be held in a cell for two to six years, hoping that his appeals will succeed, not really knowing what they are all about, but knowing that if they fail, he will be taken out and cinched down and put to death. Most of the people in prison are reasonably nice to him, and even a little apologetic; but he realizes every day for that seven hundred or twenty-one hundred days that they are holding him there helpless for the approaching slaughter; and that, once the final order is given, they will truss him up and kill him, and that nobody in that vast surrounding machinery of public officials and servants of the law will raise a finger to save him. This is why Camus once wrote that an execution . . . is not simply death. It is just as different . . . from the privation of life as a concentration camp is from prison . . . It adds to death a a public premeditation known to the future victim, an organization . . . which is itself a source of moral sufferings more terrible than death. . . . [Capital punishment] is . . . the most premeditated of murders, to which no criminal's deed, however calculated . . . , can be compared. . . . For there to be an equivalence, the death penalty would have to punish a criminal who had warned his victim of the date at which he would inflict a horrible death on him and who, from that moment onward, had confined him at his mercy for months. Such a monster is not encountered in private life.

I will spare you descriptions of the execution itself. Evelle Younger speaks to you next week, and he will probably describe some very gory, gruesome murders to you. All murders are horrible things, and executions are usually a lot cleaner physically—although, like Camus, I have never heard of a murderer who held his victim captive for two or more years waiting as the minutes and the hours ticked away toward his preannounced death. The clinical details of an execution are as unimaginable to me as they are to most of you. We have not permitted public executions in this country for over forty years. The law in every State forbids more than a few people to watch the deed done behind prison walls. Seven months ago, a federal judge in Texas ruled that executions could be photographed for television; but now the attorneys-general of twenty-five states have asked the federal Court of Appeals to set aside that ruling. I can only leave to your imagination what they are trying so very hard to hide from us. Oh, of course, executions are too hideous to put on television; we all know that. But let us not forget that it is the same hideous thing, done in secret, which we are discussing under abstract labels like "capital punishment" that permit us to talk about the subject over lunch instead of spitting up.

In any event, Mr. Younger will probably tell you about some very horrible murders, and I decline to insult your intelligence by playing "can you top this" with issues of life and death. I ask you only to remember two things, if and when you hear such descriptions.

First, the murders being described are not murders that are being done by us, or in our name, or with our approval; and our power to stop them is exceedingly limited even under the most exaggerated suppositions of deterrence, which I shall shortly return to question. Every execution, on the other hand, is done by our paid servants, in our collective name, and we can stop them all. Please do not be bamboozled into thinking that people who are against executions are in favor of murders. If we had the individual or the collective power to stop murders, we would stop them all—and for the same basic reason that we want to stop executions. Murders and executions are both ugly, vicious things, because they destroy the same sacred and mysterious gift of life which we do not understand and can never restore.

Second, please remember therefore that descriptions of murders are relevant to the subject of capital punishment only on the theory that two wrongs make a right, or that killing murderers can assuage their victims' sufferings or bring them back to life, or that capital punishment is the best deterrent to murder. The first two propositions are absurd, and the third is debatable—although, as I shall later show, the evidence is overwhelmingly against it. My present point is only that deterrence *is* debatable, whereas *we know* that persons whom we execute are dead beyond recall, no matter how the debate about deterrence comes out. That is a sufficient reason, I believe, why the burden of proof on the issue of deterrence should be placed squarely upon the executioners.

There are other reasons too. Let me try to state them briefly.

Capital punishment not merely kills people; it also kills some of them in error; and these are errors which we can never correct. When I speak about legal error, I do not mean only the question whether "they got the right man" or killed somebody who "didn't do it." Errors of that sort do occur: Timothy Evans, for example—an innocent man whose execution was among the reasons for the abolition of the death penalty in Great Britain. If you read Anthony Scaduto's recent book, *Scapegoat,* you will come away with unanswerable doubts whether Bruno Richard Hauptmann was really guilty of the kidnaping of the Lindbergh infant for which he was executed, or whether we killed Hauptmann, too, for a crime he did not commit. In 1975, the Florida Cabinet pardoned two black men, Freddie Lee Pitts and Wilbert Lee, who were twice tried and sentenced to death and spent twelve years apiece on death row for a murder committed by somebody else. This one, I am usually glibly told, "does not count," because Pitts and Lee were never actually put to death. Take comfort if you will but I cannot, for I know that only the general constitutional attack which we were then mounting upon the death penalty in Florida kept Pitts and Lee alive long enough to permit discovery of the evidence of their innocence. Our constitutional attack is now dead, and so would Pitts and Lee be if they were tried tomorrow. Sure, we catch some errors. But we often catch them by extremely lucky breaks that could as easily not have happened. I represented a young man in North Carolina who came within a hair's breadth of being the Gary Gilmore of his day. Like Gilmore, he became so depressed under a death sentence that he tried to dismiss his appeal; he was barely talked out of it; his conviction was reversed; and on retrial a jury acquitted him in eleven minutes.

We do not know how many "wrong men" have been executed. We think and pray that it is rare—although we can't be sure because, after a man is dead, people seldom continue to investigate the possibility that he was innocent. But that is not the biggest source of error anyway.

What about *legal* error? In 1968, the Supreme Court of the United States held that it was unconstitutional to exclude citizens from capital trial juries simply because they had general conscientious or religious objections to the death penalty. That decision was held retroactive; and I represented sixty or seventy men whose death sentences were subsequently set aside for constitutional errors in jury selection. While researching their cases, I found the cases of at least as many more men who had already been executed on the basis of trials infected with identical errors. Eight days ago, we finally won a decision from the Supreme Court of the United States that the death penalty is excessively harsh and therefore unconstitutional for the crime of rape. Fine, but it comes too late for the 455 men executed for rape in this country since 1930—405 of them black. In 1975, the Supreme Court held that the constitutional presumption of innocence forbids a trial judge to tell the jury that the burden of proof is on a homicide defendant to show provocation which reduces murder to manslaughter. Three weeks ago, the Court held that this decision was also retroactive. Jury charges of precisely that kind were standard forms for more than a century in many American states that punished murder with death. Can we even begin to guess how many people were unconstitutionally executed under this so-called retroactive decision?

Now what about errors of fact that go to the degree of culpability of a crime? In many States, the difference between first and second degree murder—or between capital and noncapital murder—depends on whether the defendant acted with something called "premeditation" as distinguished from intent to kill. Premeditation means intent formed beforehand, but no particular amount of time is required. Courts tell juries that premeditation "may be as instantaneous as successive thoughts in the mind." Mr. Justice Cardozo wrote that he did not understand the concept of premeditation after several decades of studying and trying to apply it as a judge. Yet this is the kind of question to which a jury's answer spells out life or death in a capital trial—this, and the questions whether the defendant had "malice aforethought," or "provocation and passion," or "insanity," or the "reasonableness" necessary for killing in self-defense. I think of another black client, Johnny Coleman, whose conviction and death sentence for killing a white truck driver named "Screwdriver" Johnson we twice got reversed by the Supreme Court of the United States. On retrial a jury acquitted him on the grounds of self-defense upon exactly the same evidence that an earlier jury had had when it sentenced him to die. When ungraspable legal standards are thus applied to intangible mental states, there is not merely the possibility but the actuarial certainty that juries deciding substantial volumes of cases are going to be wrong in an absolutely large number of them. If you accept capital punishment, you must accept the reality—not the risk, but the reality—that we shall kill people whom the law says that it is not proper to kill. No other outcome is possible when we presume to administer an infallible punishment through a fallible system.

You will notice that I have taken examples of black defendants as some of my cases of legal error. There is every reason to believe that discrimination on grounds of race and poverty fatally infects the administration of capital justice in this country. Since 1930, an almost equal number of white and black defendants has been executed for the crime of murder, although blacks constituted only about a tenth of the nation's population during this period. No sufficiently careful studies have been done of these cases, controlling other variables than race, so as to determine exactly what part race played in the outcome. But when that kind of systematic study *was* done in rape cases, it showed beyond the statistical possibility of a doubt that black men who raped white women were disproportionately sentenced to die on the basis of race alone. Are you prepared to believe that juries which succumbed to conscious or unconscious racial prejudices in rape cases were or are able to put those prejudices wholly aside where the crime charged is murder? Is it not much more plausible to believe that even the most conscientious juror—or judge, or prosecuting attorney —will be slower to want to inflict the death penalty on a defendant with whom he can identify as a human being; and that the process of identification in our society is going to be very seriously affected by racial identity? There have been two studies—one by the Stanford Law Review and the other by the Texas Judicial Council—which found no racial discrimination in capital sentencing in certain murder cases. But both of these studies had methodological problems and limitations; and both of them also found death-sentencing discrimination against the economically poor, who come disproportionately from minorities. The sum of the evidence stands where the National Crime Commission found it ten years ago, when it described the following "discriminatory patterns. The death sentence," said the Commission, "is disproportionately imposed and carried out on the poor, the Negro, and members of unpopular groups."

Apart from discrimination, there is a haphazard, crazy-quilt character about the administration of capital punishment that every knowledgeable lawyer or observer can describe but none can rationally explain. Some juries are hanging juries; some counties are hanging counties; some years are hanging years; and men live or die depending on these flukes.

However atrocious the crime may have been for which a particular defendant is sentenced to die, "[e]xperienced wardens know many prisoners serving life or less whose crimes were equally, or more atrocious." That is a quotation, by the way, from former Attorney General Ramsey Clark's statement to a congressional subcommittee; and Wardens Lewis Lawes, Clinton Duffy and others have said the same thing.

With it I come to the end of my first point. I submit that the deliberate judicial extinction of human life is intrinsically so final and so terrible an act as to cast the burden of proof for its justification upon those who want us to do it. But certainly when that act is executed through a fallible system which assures that we will kill some people wrongly, others because they are black or poor or personally ugly or socially unacceptable, and all of them quite freakishly in the sense that whether a man lives or dies for any particular crime is a matter of luck and happenstance, *then*, at the least, the burden of justifying capital punishment lies fully and heavily on its proponents.

Let us consider those justifications.

The first and the oldest is the concept of *retribution*: an eye for an eye, a life for a life. You may or may not believe in this kind of retribution, but I will not waste your time debating it because it cannot honestly be used to justify the only form of capital punishment that this country has accepted for the past half century. Even before the judicial moratorium, executions in the United States had dwindled to an average of about thirty a year. Only a rare, sparse handful of convicted murderers was being sentenced to die or executed for the self-same crimes for which many, many times as many murderers were sent away to prison. Obviously, as Herbert Wechsler said a generation ago, the issue of capital punishment is no longer "whether it is fair or just that one who takes another person's life should lose his own. . . . [W]e do not and cannot act upon . . . [that proposition] generally in the administration of the penal law. The problem rather is whether a small and highly random sample of people who commit murder . . . ought to be despatched, while most of those convicted of . . . [identical] crimes are dealt with by imprisonment."

Sometimes the concept of retribution is modernized a little with a notion called *moral reinforcement*—the idea that we should punish very serious crimes very severely in order to demonstrate how much we abhor them. The trouble with *this* justification for capital punishment, of course, is that it completely begs the question, which is *how severely* we ought to punish any particular crime to show appropriate abhorrence for it. The answer can hardly be found in a literal application of the eye-for-an-eye formula. We do not burn down arsonists' houses or cheat back at bunco artists. But if we ought not punish all crimes exactly according to their kind, then what is the fit moral reinforcement for murder? You might as well say burning at the stake or boiling in oil as simple gassing or electrocution.

Or is it not more plausible—if what we really want to say is that the killing of a human being is wrong and ought to be condemned as clearly as we can—that we should choose the punishment of prison as the fitting means to make this point? So far as moral reinforcement goes, the difference between life imprisonment and capital punishment is precisely that imprisonment continues to respect the value of human life. The plain message of capital punishment, on the other hand, is that life ceases to be sacred whenever someone with the power to take it away decides that there is a sufficiently compelling pragmatic reason to do so.

But there is still another theory of a retributive sort which is often advanced to support the death penalty, particularly in recent years. This is the argument that *we*—(that is, the person making the argument)—we no longer believe in the outworn concept of retribution; but the *public*—the great and unwashed masses of the public—*they* believe in retribution; and so we must let them have their prey or they will lose respect for law. Watch for this argument because it is the surest sign of demagogic depravity. It is disgusting in its patronizing attribution to "the public" of a primitive, uneducable bloodthirstiness which the speaker is unprepared to defend but is prepared to exploit as a means of side-stepping the rational and moral limitations of a *just* theory of retribution. It out-judases Judas in its abnegation of governmental responsibility to respond to popular misinformation with enlightenment, instead of seizing on it as a pretext for atrocity. This argument asserts that the proper way to deal with a lynch mob is to string its victim up before they do. I will say no more about it.

Another supposed justification for capital punishment that deserves equally brief treatment is the notion of *isolation* or *specific deterrence*—the idea that we must kill a murderer to prevent him from murdering ever again. The usual forms that this argument takes are that a life sentence does not mean a life sentence—it means parole after seven, or twelve, or twenty-five years—; and that, within prisons themselves, guards and other prisoners are in constant jeopardy of death at the hands of convicted but unexecuted murderers. It amazes me that these arguments can be made or taken seriously. Are we really going to kill a human being because we do not trust other people—the people whom we have chosen to serve on our own parole boards—to make a proper judgment in his case at some future time? We trust this same parole board to make far more numerous, difficult and dangerous decisions: hardly a week passes when they do not consider the cases of armed robbers, for example, although armed robbers are much, much more likely statistically to commit future murders than any murderer is to repeat his crime. But pass this point. If we refuse to trust the parole system, then let us provide by law that the murderers whose release we fear shall be given sentences of life imprisonment without parole which *do* mean life imprisonment without parole. I myself would be against that, but it is far more humane than capital punishment, and equally safe.

As for killings inside prisons, if you examine them you

will find that they are very rarely done by convicted murderers, but are almost always done by people imprisoned for crimes that no one would think of making punishable by death. Warden Lawes of Sing Sing and Governor Wallace of Alabama, among others, regularly employed murder convicts as house servants because they were among the very safest of prisoners. There are exceptions, of course; but these can be handled by adequate prison security. You cannot tell me or believe that a society which is capable of putting a man on the moon is incapable of putting a man in prison, keeping him there, and keeping him from killing while he is there. And if anyone says that this is costly, and that we should kill people in order to reduce government expenditures, I can only reply that the cost of housing a man for life in the most physically secure conditions imaginable is considerably less than the cost of putting the same man through all of the extraordinary legal proceedings necessary to kill him.

That brings me to the last supposed justification for the death penalty: *deterrence.* This is the subject that you most frequently hear debated, and many people who talk about capital punishment talk about nothing else. I have done otherwise today, partly for completeness, partly because it is vital to approach the subject of deterrence knowing precisely what question you want to ask and have answered. I have suggested that the proper question is *whether there is sufficiently convincing evidence that the death penalty deters murder better than does life imprisonment so that you are willing to accept responsibility for doing the known evil act of killing human beings—with all of the attending uglinesses that I have described—on the faith of your conviction in the superior deterrent efficacy of capital punishment.*

If this is the question, then I submit that there is only one fair and reasonable answer. When the Supreme Court of the United States reviewed the evidence last year, it described that evidence as "inconclusive." Do not let Evelle Younger or anybody else tell you that the Supreme Court held the death penalty justifiable as a deterrent. What the Court's plurality opinion said, exactly, was that "there is no convincing evidence *either supporting or refuting* . . . [the] view" that "the death penalty may not function as a significantly greater deterrent than lesser penalties." *Because* the evidence was inconclusive, the Court held that the Constitution did not forbid judgment either way. But if the evidence is inconclusive, is it your judgment that we should conclusively kill people on a factual theory that the evidence does not conclusively sustain?

I hope not. But let us examine the evidence more carefully because—even though it is not conclusive—it is very, very substantial; and the overwhelming weight of it refutes the claims of those who say that capital punishment is a better deterrent than life imprisonment for murder.

For more than forty years, criminologists have studied this

question by a variety of means. They have compared homicide rates in countries and States that did and did not have capital punishment, or that actually executed people more and less frequently. Some of these studies compared large aggregates of abolitionist and retentionist States; others compared geographically adjacent pairs or triads of States, or States that were chosen because they were comparable in other socio-economic factors that might affect homicide. Other studies compared homicide rates in the same country or State before and after the abolition or reinstatement of capital punishment; or homicide rates for the same geographic area during periods preceding and following well-publicized executions. Special comparative studies were done relating to police killings and prison killings. All in all, there were dozens of studies. Without a single exception, *none* of them found that the death penalty had any statistically significant effect upon the rate of homicide or murder. Often I have heard advocates of capital punishment explain away its failures by likening it to a great lighthouse: "We count the ships that crash," they say, "but we never know how many saw the light and were saved." What these studies show, however, is that coastlines of the same shape and depth and tidal structure, with and without lighthouses, invariably have the same number of shipwrecks per year. On that evidence, would you invest your money in a lighthouse, or would you buy sonar if you really wanted to save lives?

In 1975, the first purportedly scientific study ever to find that capital punishment *did* deter homicides was published. This was done by Isaac Ehrlich of Chicago, who is not a criminologist but an economist. Using regression analysis involving an elaborate mathematical model, Ehrlich reported that every execution deterred something like eight murders. Naturally, supporters of capital punishment hurriedly clambered on the Ehrlich bandwagon.

Unhappily for them, the wagon was a factory reject. Several distinguished econometricians—including a team headed by Lawrence Klein, president of the American Economic Association—reviewed Ehrlich's work and found it fatally flawed with numerous methodological errors. Some of these were technical: it appeared, for example, that Ehrlich had produced his results by the unjustified and unexplained use of a logarithmic form of regression equation instead of the more conventional linear form—which made his findings of deterrence vanish. Equally important, it was shown that Ehrlich's findings depended entirely on data from the post-1962 period, when executions declined and the homicide rate rose *as a part of a general rise in the over-all crime rate that Ehrlich incredibly failed to consider.* Incidentally, the non-scientific proponents of capital punishment are also fond of suggesting that the rise in homicide rates in the 1960's and the 1970's, when executions were halted, proves that executions used to deter homicides. This is ridiculous when you consider that crime as a whole has increased during this period; that homicide rates have increased about *half* as much as the rates for all other F.B.I. Index crimes; and that whatever factors are affecting the rise of most non-capital crimes (which *cannot* include cessation of executions) almost certainly affect the homicide-rate rise also.

In any event, Ehrlich's study was discredited; and a second, methodologically inferior study by a fellow named Yunker is not even worth criticizing here. These are the only two scientific studies in forty years, I repeat, which have ever purported to find deterrence. On the other hand, several recent studies have been completed by researchers who adopted Ehrlich's basic regression-analysis approach but corrected its defects. Peter Passell did such a study finding no deterrence. Kenneth Avio did such a study finding no deterrence. Brian Forst did such a study finding no deterrence. If you want to review all of these studies yourselves, you may find them discussed and cited in an excellent article that just appeared in the 1976 *Supreme Court Review* by Hans Zeisel, at page 317. The conclusion you will have to draw is that—during forty years and today—the scientific community has looked and looked and looked for any reliable evidence that capital punishment deters homicide better than life imprisonment; and it has found no such evidence at all.

Next week Evelle Younger will probably tell you about a different kind of study: one that was done by the Los Angeles Police Department. Police officers asked arrested robbers who did not carry guns, or did not use them, *why* they did not; and the answers, supposedly, were frequently that the robber "did not want to get the death penalty." It is noteworthy that the Los Angeles Police Department has consistently refused to furnish copies of this study and its underlying data to professional scholars, apparently for fear of criticism. I finally obtained a copy of the study from a legislative source, and I can tell you that it shows two things. First, an arrested person will tell a police officer anything that he thinks the officer wants to hear. Second, police officers—like all other human beings—hear what we want to hear. When a robber tries to say that he did not carry or use a gun because he did not wish to risk the penalties for homicide, he will describe those penalties in terms of whatever the law happens to be at that time and place. In Minnesota, which has no death penalty, he will say "I didn't want to get life imprisonment." In Los Angeles, he will say "I didn't want to get the death penalty." Both responses mean the same thing; neither tells you that death is a superior deterrent to life imprisonment.

The real mainstay of the deterrence thesis, however, is not evidence but intuition. You and I ask ourselves: are we not afraid to die? Of course! Would the threat of death, then, not intimidate us to forbear from a criminal act? Certainly! *Therefore*, capital punishment must be a deterrent. The trouble with this intuition is that the people who are doing the reasoning and the people who are doing the murdering are not the same people. You and I do not commit murder for a lot of reasons other than the death penalty. The death penalty might perhaps also deter us from murdering—but altogether needlessly, since we would not murder with it or without it. Those who are sufficiently dissocialized to murder are not responding to the world in the way that we are; and we simply cannot "intuit" their thinking processes from ours.

Consider, for example, the well-documented cases of persons who kill *because* there is a death penalty. One of these was Pamela Watkins, a baby sitter in San Jose who had made several unsuccessful suicide attempts and was frightened to try again. She finally strangled two children so that the State of California would execute her. In various bizarre forms, this "suicide-murder" syndrome is reported by psychiatrists again and again. (Parenthetically, Gary Gilmore was probably such a case.) If you intuit that somewhere, sometime, the death penalty *does* deter some potential murderers, are you also prepared to intuit that their numbers mathematically exceed the numbers of these wretched people who are actually induced to murder by the existence of capital punishment?

Here, I suggest, our intuition does—or should—fail, just as the evidence certainly does fail, to establish a deterrent justification for the death penalty. There is simply no credible evidence, and there is no rational way of reasoning about the real facts once you know them, which can sustain this or any other justification with the degree of confidence that should be demanded before a civilized society deliberately extinguishes human life.

I have only a little time for my final point, but it is sufficient because the point is perfectly plain. Capital punishment is a dying institution in this last quarter of the Twentieth Century. It has already been abandoned in law or in fact throughout most of the civilized world. England, Canada, the Scandinavian countries, virtually all of Western Europe except for France and Spain, have abolished the death penalty. The vast majority of countries in the Western Hemisphere have abolished it. Its last strongholds in the world—apart from the United States—are in Asia and Africa, particularly South Africa. Even the countries which maintain capital punishment on the books have almost totally ceased to use it in fact. In the United States, considering only the last half-century, executions have plummeted from 199 in 1935 to approximately 29 a year during the decade before 1967, when the ten-year judicial moratorium began.

Do you doubt that this development will continue? Do you doubt that it will continue because it is the path of civilization—the path up out of fear and terror and the barbarism that terror breeds, into self-confidence and decency in the administration of justice? The road, like any other built by men, has its detours; but over many generations it has run true, and will run true. And there will therefore come a time— perhaps in twenty years, perhaps in fifty or a hundred, but very surely and very shortly as the lifetime of nations is measured— when our children will look back at us in horror and un- belief because of what we did in their names and for their supposed safety, just as we look back in horror and unbelief at the thousands of crucifixions and beheadings and live disembowelments that our ancestors practiced for the sup- posed purpose of making our world safe from murderers and robbers, thieves, shoplifters, and pickpockets. All of these kinds of criminals are still with us, and will still be with our children—although we can certainly decrease their numbers and their damage, and protect ourselves from them a lot better, if we insist that our politicians stop pounding on the whipping boy of capital punishment and start coming up with some real solutions to the real problems of crime. Our children will cease to execute murderers for the same reason that we have ceased to string up pickpockets and shoplifters at the public crossroads, although there are still plenty of them around. Our children will cease to execute murderers because executions are a self- deluding, self-defeating, self-degrading, futile and entirely stupid means of dealing with the crime of murder, and because our children will prefer to be something better than murderers themselves. Should we not—can we not—make the same choice now?

CAPITAL PUNISHMENT
EVELLE J. YOUNGER

I think people feel strongly about capital punishment. I rarely meet someone who says I don't know how I feel about capital punishment. I usually meet someone whose mind is made up for one reason or another. In that connection, I think people are for or against capital punishment for different rea- sons, some are valid, some are not. I'd like to explore some of those reasons, particularly some of those I suggest are invalid. I don't mind people disagreeing with me on this position. I do mind people disagreeing with me for improper reason.

For example, the old question—punishment of "an eye for an eye." That attitude in support of capital punishment has

"Capital Punishment" by Evelle J. Younger. From Vital Speeches of the Day, vol. 43, no. 22, Sept. 1, 1977. Reprinted by permission of the publisher, City News Publishing Co., Southold, N.Y.

generally fallen into disrepute. If you believe that just punishing someone is good enough reason for capital punishment, you don't go around in polite circles saying so. The fact is that I've known a few people willing to admit that's their motivation.

Often a person's attitude about capital punishment has something to do with their own personal experience. The Bible can be used to support either position you want to take. You can find just about as many quotations to support opposition to capital punishment as you can to support an attitude in favor of capital punishment.

So far as I'm concerned, I'm human enough to think my position in support of capital punishment is the valid one, and simply stated, has to do with cost. For a million years, we've been trying to control human behavior by applying a certain formula. Every human institution, whether you're talking about a government of 22 million people as we have in California, or a high school football team, or a Sunday school class, or whatever. Whatever you're operating, if you're trying to control behavior, you do it by, number one, establishing ground rules; number two, setting up a procedure to determine when someone violates a ground rule. In other words, try them—are they guilty or innocent, and if they're guilty, if they've violated the ground rules, punishing them. That's the way you raise children. That's the way we try to handle dangerous violent criminals. But there has to be some logical connection between the offense and the cost.

A few years ago, I strongly supported an amendment to the law making the sale of heroin a mandatory prison sentence, because absent that mandatory prison sentence, 80 percent of those who sold heroin were getting probation. And it's a little hard being Attorney General charged with the responsibility of enforcing laws relating to the sale of heroin, if those violating the law get probation in four out of five cases. The price isn't high enough in other words to discourage someone who wants to go into the business of selling heroin.

Ditto absent capital punishment, the price for killing someone under certain circumstances isn't high enough. For example, absent capital punishment, there is no reason for a rapist to leave his victim alive. Because a rape calls for life imprisonment, absent capital punishment, murder calls for the penalty of life imprisonment. So the rapist can murder his victim and eliminate a witness, and increase his chances of avoiding successful prosecution, all secure in the knowledge that if he is caught and punished, he hasn't increased the price of his crime one whit.

Ditto a person who holds up a filling station, and binds and gags the attendant. Absent capital punishment, there's no reason for the gunman to not execute the attendant. I'd like to give the gunman a reason for leaving the attendant bound, gagged and alive on the floor of the filling station.

That's my rationalization. That's my reason for strongly supporting capital punishment. I don't believe the death penalty will deter all murders. It won't even deter most murders. It will deter, in my firm opinion, some murders. And, when you're talking about deterring the murder of innocent people, I don't think you have to deal in thousands before you can justify what I believe to be a very realistic penalty.

And I'm also aware that 75 percent of the people in California believe the death penalty is a protection which they need and are entitled to. Now, this question is not subject to any scientific analysis; not something one person knows a great deal about and another person knows nothing about. You can't come up with a right answer by using a slide rule. Everyone in this room, and most of the citizens in this state are just as well qualified to arrive at a correct conclusion in this as I am, or as is Professor Amsterdam, or as is Governor Brown. This is not something that's subject to expert testimony, I think every citizen has a stake in this and the fact 75 percent of our citizens support the reenactment of the death penalty is significant. Also, statistics are relevant, not conclusive, but relevant. The courts abolished capital punishment in California in 1963. There's been one execution since then. Since then, the murder rate has tripled in California. From 1954 to 1963, the murder rate was three to four per one hundred thousand. It skyrocketed to over 10.4 per one hundred thousand in the last couple years.

In 1975, 2196 willful homicides occurred, as compared to 666 in 1963.

Those who oppose capital punishment will say so what, crime has gone up during this same period. That's true. And I think the reason is precisely the same. We were just as unrealistic dealing with rapists and robbers as we were in dealing with murderers.

In the 60s and early 70s it was every man to his own supreme court. We went through a period here where young people, if they wanted to improve the educational system they were attending, they would try to burn down the administration building. We rationalized an awful lot of weird conduct during the 60s and this was the period when we made it financially attractive for local authorities to put people on probation.

We did a lot of foolish things, like amending the law in 1965 to remove all restrictions on the grant of probation. It was a turbulent period, and the fact crime generally went up proves to me we we weren't dealing with crime very realistically.

As I've indicated, I want to identify some of those reasons for opposing capital punishment that I regard as unsupportable. I just think the arguments are not valid. For example, one of the favorite arguments for anyone who opposes capital punishment is that it really doesn't have public support. If people were asked a question by someone taking a poll, they'll say 'I'm for capital punishment,' but if they're put on a jury where they have to act on it as a juror or a private citizen, they don't really support the concept.

That argument is absolutely and completely untrue. It's rather remarkable that the argument was stated so forcefully by our own state Supreme Court in 1972. They said in an attempt to rationalize their legislatively abolishing the death penalty in California, that although death penalty statutes remain on the books of many jurisdictions, the frequency of its application suggests that among persons called upon to carry out the death penalty, it's being repudiated with ever increasing frequency.

Well, that decision is certainly an interesting piece of social legislation, but as a legal document it falls far short of the usual high standards set by our Supreme Court.

Capital punishment has been infrequently applied because Appellate Courts have repeatedly interfered. In 1972, when the California Supreme Court struck down this state's death penalty, 107 persons whom judges or juries had sentenced to death, including Charles Manson and Sirhan Sirhan, were spared. In that same year, the United States Supreme Court invalidated the as then applied death penalty laws nationwide, and approximately 600 persons under sentence of death could not be executed.

Before the California Supreme Court again struck down this last law in December of 1976, approximately 69 additional persons had been condemned to die. Therefore, it's hard to see how anybody could conclude the death penalty lacks public support.

We pointed out in our brief before the California Supreme Court in 1972, accepting for the purpose of argument that the Court's explanation that the delay in execution rendered the death penalty unconstitutional as cruel punishment, can it be assumed that had this court not permitted and caused excessive delay, the death penalty would therefore be constitutional? If so, it's not society's standards of decency that transform capital punishment from constitutional to unconstitutional. It's the procrastination that this court has built into our system of criminal justice.

Another false concept that's been foisted on substantial portions of our population relates to the concept that only the poor and friendless get the death penalty. Of course, the argument that juries are likely to inflict the death penalty on the indigent rather than the wealthy is just not valid.

Under California's death penalty law struck down last December, the death penalty was possible only for those first degree murderers in which aggravating special circumstances occurred, such as hired killings, killing more than one person, killing while committing rape, child molesting, kidnapping, robbery or burglary, killing a witness to prevent his testimony, or killing a peace officer in line of duty where proved beyond a reasonable doubt.

Seven of the inmates on death row were there because they

agreed to pay others to commit murders. The occupations of the 69 persons on death row at that time were seven owners of businesses, one housewife, 35 skilled workers, eleven laborers, 12 unemployed and three unknown. Makes it pretty clear that California's judges and juries haven't been concerned just with the occupation or economic status of the killer in applying the death penalty.

They've really concentrated on the aggravated nature of the murder instead. I think it's also significant that of those 69 on death row, when the decision commuted their sentences to life imprisonment, 24 were on death row because they had killed a witness to avoid prosecution for some other crime. It's true there are not many millionaires on death row. That's true but not valid, because millionaires do not commit crimes that rate a position on death row. Millionaires do not hold up filling stations and execute the attendant.

Those who think someone like Dr. Finch and Carol Tregoff escaped the death penalty because of their financial and social position overlook the fact that no matter how poor an individual, nobody in that kind of triangular emotional sort of thing goes to death row. Nobody makes it to death row by killing a wife or husband or sweetheart, unless they do it for pay.

Only in the Soviet Union, among the major countries today, is an economic crime punishable by death, and even there, while they have such a law on the books, they have not applied the law for many years.

Another argument, a favorite of those who oppose the death penalty, is that we can accomplish the same thing by life imprisonment without possibility of parole. There are several things wrong with that. There is no such thing in our nation or in our state as true life imprisonment, nor should there be.

The governor has, and always should have, the power to commute. In any civilized system, the chief executive has to have the power to pardon. That's the safety valve that will work when everything else fails. So I wouldn't be in favor of, if we could, and it would be impossible, to try and take away the governor's power to commute. Given that power to commute, there's no such thing as life imprisonment. You simply substitute the governor's clemency hearing for a parole hearing now.

But eventually a person who goes into prison for sentence other than the death penalty will likely get out.

If you're the victim of an individual once sentenced to death and later paroled, you're not concerned with large numbers, you're just concerned with the outrageousness that a person who has demonstrated the willingness to commit cold blooded murder could be treated with unrealistic tension.

Also, another argument for not having in your system the concept of life imprisonment without parole is that there is always the possibility of escape. Now those who favor life imprisonment without possibility of parole minimize that.

There's one other reason why life without possibility of

parole is not a realistic alternative, and that is that you cannot run a prison without giving those in prison some hope of eventual release. Heavens knows it's bad enough in prison now. If everyone in San Quentin knows that someday he's going to get out, and yet they still cut each other up and do terrible things over there, can you imagine what life imprisonment would be like if no one there had any hope of release? If everyone in prison, or even a substantial portion, were there literally for life, there'd be no way you could maintain any degree of order.

The one thing that makes most prison communities manageable now is the fact that the vast majority of persons are on good behavior looking forward to that day when someone says, "O.K., we're going to put you on parole."

Of course, there are arguments to the effect that mistakes are always possible, and if a person is executed there is no way to correct the mistake. Well, maybe. But as a practical matter, under our system in California today, it's impossible, inconceivable that an innocent person would ever be executed.

The system tilts heavily, and properly so, in favor of a person accused of crimes. We have so many checks and protections now that didn't exist 20 years ago. The problem today is not that we are going to convict an innocent person of murder, the problem is how do you convict those that are admittedly guilty? The Supreme Court in its landmark cases for the past 25 years has virtually no concern for guilt or innocence. It's been referred to sneeringly as the irrelevance of guilt when talking about the American system. The fact is, I selected 25 landmark cases of the Supreme Court in the last 25 years, and only in two cases did the court express any doubt as to the guilt of the defendants. In the other 23 cases where they reversed the trial court's convictions, they did so because of procedural matters. They assumed the guilt; acknowledged the guilt of the defendant. So, I say, as a practical matter, the possibility of an innocent person being executed for murder is completely unrealistic and unsupportable by any facts.

One thing I might mention with regard to the question of capital punishment: in case the governor's veto stands, I along with most of the heads of statewide law enforcement organizations, along with a number of distinguished lawmakers, will take a leadership role in getting the initiative on the ballot to give you and the other citizens of the state the chance to again express your support of the death penalty. I hope that isn't necessary. I hope that we can override the governor's veto, in which case the death penalty will be restored immediately. And I think it should be.

The death penalty is not the kind of thing you play political games with. I believe the death penalty is a protection people need. I believe the death penalty will save lives, so I'd like to have it restored as soon as possible. If we cannot override the governor's veto, it's going to be November of 1978 before we can get it on the ballot and the death penalty can be restored.

Now, in the meantime, there are going to be some innocent people killed, and some of those innocent people could have conceivably been spared, given the fact the death penalty might have been in effect at that time.

This brings me to the final point I'd like to emphasize. I think we don't want to forget why we're going through this traumatic experience now. We went through it in 1972, now we're going through it again. It's a frightfully emotional and traumatic experience for an individual or for a state. We shouldn't have to be doing this except for a sub-par performance on the part of the Supreme Court. I am not talking about the failure of a particular justice to arrive at a proper result. I'm talking about the institutional failure of the court. You can demonstrate it in several ways. Let's compare their conduct in regard to the death penalty with what I conceive to be their institutional failure.

In 1972, the United States Supreme Court said the death penalty is constitutional, but only if you make it mandatory. If you don't make it mandatory, we're afraid you might apply it in an arbitrary or indiscriminate fashion, and we don't want you to do that. I won't pretend that there weren't unanswered questions in respect to that decision, because all nine members wrote opinions about that decision. Not many would have passed the kind of examination your tenth-grade youngster gets in an English class. But you see, there's no one to give a report card to the members of the United States Supreme Court. They can be illogical. They can write confusing and unrealistic decisions, and there's nobody to tell them they did. They are supreme, and there's no one more supreme.

I suggest it was somewhat of a confused issue. The fact is the message came through loud and clear. If you want a death penalty, it has to be mandatory.

They made it mandatory in California and a number of other states, and last December the Supreme Court changed its mind, and said, well, the death penalty is still constitutional, but only if you give the judge and jury some discretion. It was a 180-degree turnaround. They simply changed their minds. That's why I say it's a part of the institutional failure of the Supreme Court.

The court has also legislated in a large number of cases. The Miranda decision produced detailed admonition during interrogation procedures. A series of Fourth Amendment exclusionary rule cases established a detailed code of conduct in police procedures. And for the last twenty years, obscenity cases involved the Supreme Court sitting as a standardless board of censors. And that's been a complete failure. I suggest that their biggest institutional failure has been that they've gotten into areas that are properly areas for the legislature. The courts are not set up properly to legislate. They can't hold hearings, they can't seek out evidence. They've got to deal with what they have before them. They've got to wait for a case.

The legislature, if it makes a mistake, can correct it during the next session. The court has to wait, maybe years, for a factual situation, before they can change their mind. The institutional failures, I suggest, are rooted in the institution's designs, not in the fault of a few maverick judges. So in closing, I'd like to suggest to you that you consider, and I'm considering it, changing the Constitution to provide for a 12- to 16-year fixed term for a Supreme Court Justice; long enough to provide necessary insulation against political foul weather, long enough to allow the justices to develop and expound the theory of jurisprudence, but short enough to ensure the court members are not entirely out of touch with the times.

If this sounds outrageous and sinful, remember one of the successes of our nation over the past 200 years has been due to the fact we are able to give somebody almost unlimited authority and then take it back.

After Franklin D. Roosevelt served for more than 3 terms, despite his great popularity, we decided it wasn't a good idea, so in the early 50's we passed an amendment limiting the term of a president.

We've done that with the military. We've surrounded our military leaders, in the last few generations, with considerably more restraint and restriction than ever existed before. I think we could properly do that with the Supreme Court. I think it's worth your consideration. A group of your size and prestige might well have an impact upon the thinking of a large number of people in that connection.

QUESTIONS FOR DISCUSSION

1. In what ways are the two speeches, in combination, like a symposium? In what ways are they like a debate? In what ways are they different from discussion or debate?

2. Can you word the topic as a debate topic? As a discussion question? What are some of the advantages and disadvantages of each?

3. If you were having a discussion on this topic, what solutions could you suggest?

4. What are the major kinds of logic used in the speeches? How are they developed?

5. What are the major emotional appeals? How are they developed?

6. These speeches do not follow all the steps given in the motivated sequences for persuasive speeches discussed in Part 3 of this text. Why?

7. Can you think of other topics or problems that could be discussed in a debate, a symposium, or a panel discussion?

10

USING THE
SYMPOSIUM

When a group that you belong to calls on you to organize the discussion of a group problem, you will want to consider using the symposium. In a symposium, each of several speakers is asked to give a prepared speech on some aspect of the problem or on one possible solution. The speeches are followed by a forum, during which the speakers respond to questions and comments from the audience. The group as a whole, speakers and listeners, discusses the proposals and selects what seems on the basis of available information to be the best one.

The symposium is the most formal type of group discussion, but it is usually the easiest to plan, and it offers the best chance for full consideration of all important aspects of a problem and possible solutions. It is a good way to begin your study of group discussion, because it allows you to research and prepare most of your portion of the discussion in advance and to become familiar with the basic steps in problem solving.

ASSIGNMENT

With a group of three to five of your classmates, examine some of your common problems. They may be international, national, local, school, or personal problems. Select a problem that you all agree is important for each of you, and plan a symposium-forum discussion of it. (See Chapter 16 for additional suggestions on interpersonal and small-group discussions.)

STATEMENT OF PROBLEM

State your problem in the form of a question, phrasing the question in such a way that it will lead to open-minded consideration of all the possible solutions. Avoid questions like "Should the electoral system be abolished?" which would lead to a yes-or-no debate on one solution. If you wish to discuss this problem, the question should be worded, "What is the best method of electing the President of the United States?" That way all solutions can be considered, their advantages and disadvantages discussed, and the best one selected.

Here are some other examples:

How can the United States best assist in the development of the new nations of Africa?

How can we eliminate racial discrimination in housing?

How can cheating in the classroom be prevented?

How could academic counseling be improved?

How much responsibility should the college take for the sexual conduct of its students?

ORGANIZATION

First, organize your group. One of the members must be chosen discussion leader or moderator. It will be his or her job to introduce the problem and the speakers; to keep the discussion moving toward its goal in an orderly fashion by, for example, asking questions if things slow down and bringing the discussion back to the topic if it drifts off toward side issues; and to state the conclusions the group has reached. He or she should be an excellent organizer who is also courteous and tactful. Select him or her carefully, because an excellent leader is essential for an excellent discussion.

The other members of the group will be speakers. Each will present a prepared speech on an aspect of the problem or the possible solutions.

Now plan the overall organization of the discussion. The format should be: (1) speeches, (2) discussion by speakers, (3) forum with audience. Assigning a topic to each speaker is properly the job of the discussion leader, but you will get the best results if you meet as a group and plan it together. The speeches and discussion should follow the five basic steps of problem solving:

1. State and define the problem.

2. Set forth criteria for a solution.

3. Present all possible solutions.

4. Discuss each solution, weighing advantages and disadvantages.

5. Select the best solution.

Probably the best—and simplest—way to organize your symposium is to have the discussion leader present the problem and criteria for a solution, and then to have each group member give a speech on one possible solution. The organizational pattern of these speeches would be like those on capital punishment reprinted at the beginning of this section of your text. Another good format is to have each speaker explain the problem and the possible solutions from his or her own viewpoint. This can be especially effective if the speakers have very different backgrounds, occupations, or philosophies. The danger is too much repetition, which is boring for the audience and can leave the final speaker with nothing to say. To avoid that, the speakers should get together to compare outlines and, where there is duplication, come to an agreement about who will cover what material.

The speeches should take up about half the time allotted for the total discussion. Most of the remaining time should be devoted to a forum in which speakers and audience participate. The forum should be an informal discussion: members of the audience direct questions to the group or to specific speakers, and audience and speakers talk over additional solutions, additional advantages or disadvantages of the solutions, agreement or disagreement with the advantages and disadvantages presented, and so forth.

The discussion leader must also allow himself or herself a few minutes (about five minutes out of an hour discussion) at the end for a summary and conclusions. In these closing remarks, he or she summarizes briefly the major points made during the symposium and the forum and presents the general feeling of the group. The moderator does not argue his or her own point of view; he or she tells the group in an objective but friendly and informal way what *its* point of view seems to be.

Although most symposium-forums do not differ significantly from the suggested plan, it is possible that your group will decide on a somewhat different allocation of material or time. The organization given here should at least serve as a starting point, but you may modify it if your topic or the composition of your group suggests a different arrangement.

DEVELOPMENT

If you are the group leader, you will find that the development of a symposium is similar to the development of the persuasive speech. First you (or the group members in their prepared speeches) must state the problem clearly, define important words, and show the nature and extent of the problem with examples, statistics, facts, and testimony. Then you (or they) should present criteria for an acceptable solution. Be objective and thorough: try to include all the characteristics that an acceptable solution would have. For example, criteria for the solution to a social problem might include effectiveness, practicality, low cost, and popular support. Prepare the list of criteria carefully, and use it later to test the solutions proposed. In developing possible solutions, present all the important advantages and disadvantages of each solution and support them with examples, facts, statistics, and testimony.

If you are a speaker, you will find that there are two major differences between a symposium and a persuasive speech. First, since each speaker is concerned with only one aspect of the topic, he or she needs to research in depth only that one aspect. However, he or she must also do some general research on the problem and on other solutions so that he or she can participate intelligently in the forum. It would be wise to take notes on all aspects of the problem and the solutions as you do your research.

The second (and most important) difference between this kind of discussion and the persuasive speech is that its purpose is not to persuade but to inform. The goal of a symposium is to put all the essential facts and information before the audience, so that the audience can make an intelligent decision. This is why leader and speakers must present the problem and propose solutions as objectively as possible, giving all the arguments on both sides. If you visualize the results of a solution, as you do in a persuasive speech, do it impartially. And eliminate the final step in persuasion, the appeal for action.

At this point you should reread and analyze the two problem-solving speeches at the beginning of Part 4 (page 205).

The outline form for this assignment covers the discussion as a whole. Use sections I, II, and III for planning the overall organization and development during your meetings with the group leader and other speakers. On a separate sheet, make a detailed outline of your portion of the symposium. Your outlines for the last two assignments can be used as a guide, but the precise form your talk takes will depend on which format your group has chosen for its symposium. Then use sections IV and V to record points made during the speeches and the group discussion that follows. Hand in the outline form, and the detailed outline of your own speech, immediately after the discussion. Give the instructor's evaluation sheet to your instructor in advance, for his or her use during your presentation.

PRACTICE

Practice your assigned speech for the symposium in the same way that you practiced the prepared speeches you gave earlier in the course. It is easier to maintain spontaneity if the discussion is not rehearsed, but it would be wise for your group to get together and talk things over shortly before the presentation. At this time you can share some of the material you have found on other aspects of the topic than the one your speech covers, and you can check to be sure that other speakers are not covering your material and you are not covering theirs. You should probably not practice delivering your speech for the other symposium members, but comparing and discussing your outlines should be helpful.

DELIVERY

In the delivery of your prepared speech and your contributions to the forum, show the same eagerness to communicate that you show in animated conversation with your friends. Throughout the discussion, carry out your own responsibilities and help others carry out theirs. To summarize those responsibilities:

The group leader (1) gives a prepared speech introducing the problem; (2) tells the audience briefly what the format of the symposium will be; and (3) introduces the speakers, plans the allocation of time and holds the group to it so that all solutions can be adequately discussed and time will be left for conclusions, asks questions to encourage discussion or clarify points, keeps the discussion on the topic, encourages balanced participation by tactfully quieting some people and inviting others to comment, and summarizes main points and conclusions at the end. Group discussions are hard to follow, partly because of the many participants and partly because members of the audience must try to make logical points on the spur of the moment. Without a good summary, the audience may think the discussion has been a pointless waste of time; with a good summary, they are likely to find that they made more valid points and progressed further toward a solution than they thought they had. The summary should review the solutions offered, the major arguments for and against them, and the amount of support for each. It is a very important part of the symposium.

The group members should be prepared with thoroughly researched and carefully practiced speeches so that they can effectively inform the audience on each aspect of the problem. During the discussion, both they and the members of the audience should participate. Each person should make his or her views known, being careful not to take more than his or her fair share of time. Courtesy and tact are called for. Speak only when called on by the discussion leader, and be sure to criticize arguments, not people.

OUTLINE: USING THE SYMPOSIUM

I THE PROBLEM

(Show how the problem developed and use examples, statistics, facts, and testimony to establish the size and scope of the problem)

OUTLINE: USING THE SYMPOSIUM

II CRITERIA FOR SOLUTION

(Show all necessary characteristics of a satisfactory solution)

OUTLINE: USING THE SYMPOSIUM

III   SUGGESTED SOLUTIONS

(List all possible solutions)

OUTLINE: USING THE SYMPOSIUM

IV DISCUSSION

(List arguments for and against each solution, and test each solution against the criteria)

OUTLINE: USING THE SYMPOSIUM

V CONCLUSIONS

(Indicate the amount of acceptance for each solution and summarize the major reasons given for accepting or rejecting the solution)

1. All favored this solution:

Reasons:

2. Most favored this solution:

Reasons:

OUTLINE: USING THE SYMPOSIUM

3. Many favored this solution:

Reasons:

4. Few favored this solution:

Reasons:

5. No one favored this solution:

Reasons:

NOTE: To be handed in after the discussion

INSTRUCTOR'S EVALUATION: USING THE SYMPOSIUM

1. **Material**

	Excellent	Good	Fair	Poor
A. Preparation				
B. Clarity of ideas				
C. Use of supporting materials				

2. **Language**

A. Vocabulary				
B. Sentence structure				

3. **Delivery**

A. Voice				
B. Enthusiasm				
C. Poise				
D. Appearance				
E. Eye contact				
F. Tact				
G. Participation				

INSTRUCTOR'S EVALUATION: USING THE SYMPOSIUM

4. Comments

GRADE _____   INSTRUCTOR _____

11

USING THE PANEL

The most popular type of group discussion is the panel, sometimes called a round-table discussion. It can be described as a planned conversation.

Participating in a panel requires you to research carefully all aspects of a problem and its possible solutions, because you will be involved in the discussion throughout. The informality of a panel is appealing, and the on-the-spot thinking and communicating that it requires make it challenging as well. Like the symposium, the panel should be followed by a forum in which the audience members take part, discussing various solutions and selecting the best one. (See Chapter 16 for suggestions on interpersonal and small-group communication.)

ASSIGNMENT

With a group of four to eight members of the class, examine some of your common problems and select one that you feel is an important problem for all of you. Plan a panel-forum discussion of this problem.

STATEMENT OF PROBLEM

State the problem in the form of a question that will lead to open inquiry and consideration of all possible solutions. In selecting your problem and stating it as a question, think about the discussions conducted for the last assignment. What kinds of problems were most interesting, and which led to the best forums?

PRELIMINARY PREPARATION

Meet together as a group and select a discussion leader. Choose carefully, because his or her leadership ability may determine the direction and quality of your discussion. Then discuss your problem. Begin by defining the problem and the words used in stating it. The members of the panel should agree on definitions, but there must be enough controversy about solutions to stimulate discussion. Talk over the possible solutions, and the support available for each through research, observation, and interviews. If you think factual support may be hard to come by, redefine your problem or choose a different one. A panel discussion that consists of unsupported opinions is little more than a pooling of ignorance.

ORGANIZATION

Plan to present the panel discussion during the first half of your class hour and to call for audience participation in a forum during the second half.

Once again, the discussion should proceed in an orderly fashion through the five steps of problem solving:

1. State and define the problem.

2. Set forth criteria for a solution.

3. Present all possible solutions.

4. Discuss each solution, weighing advantages and disadvantages.

5. Select the best solution.

DEVELOPMENT

It is sometimes thought that preparing for a discussion is easier than preparing a speech. This is not the case. Preparing for a discussion requires exhaustive research on all aspects of a problem and on all its possible solutions.

If you are a panel member (rather than the leader), begin your preparation as you would for a speech. Examine first the information you already have at hand. What do you know from your own experience and observations about the nature and importance of the problem? What would a solution have to offer in order to be acceptable to you and to the

242

people you know? What solutions would you propose? What solutions have you heard others propose? What advantages and disadvantages are you aware of for each solution? What evidence (examples, facts, and testimony) do you have to support the advantages and disadvantages? Write this information down on the outline form for this assignment.

Then begin your research, using books and magazines, observation, and interviews with experts to check the accuracy of your information and to gather the additional information you need. Add this to your outline, being sure to note the source of each bit of information.

Form some tentative conclusions based on the material you have organized, but keep an open mind. Remember that the objective of the actual discussion is the *cooperative* solution of the problem. You should not go into the discussion with your mind already made up and try to persuade the group to accept your conclusions. The other participants may present ideas that have not occurred to you. In order to take full advantage of the group process, you need to be able to consider those ideas fairly and weigh them against your own without bias.

If you are the discussion leader, study all aspects of the problem and its possible solutions so that you can bring into the discussion any important facts and ideas that the panel overlooks. But try to avoid drawing even tentative conclusions yourself. You must be impartial in dealing with ideas and people. On the outline for this assignment, make notes of ideas that should be brought out in the discussion and word them as impartial questions or statements that you can use to introduce the ideas if they are not forthcoming from the panel.

The leader of a panel should behave rather like a judge during a trial—more informal and friendly than a judge, of course, but just as objective and unbiased. As leader, you should never state your personal opinions. Instead of saying "I think X should be done," say "I have heard X suggested" or "in an article I read, the author suggested X" or "at one of our meetings, a member of the panel mentioned X." The audience and the panel should never be able to determine your personal feelings on a controversial point.

Make a tentative schedule that allows time for discussion on each of the five steps in problem solving. Give yourself about five minutes at the beginning so that you can present the problem briefly and introduce the panel, and about five minutes at the end for your summary and conclusion. When you introduce the members of the panel, try to say something about each speaker's interest in or experience with the problem. Don't use material that the speaker will want to contribute to the discussion himself or herself; instead, mention qualifications and abilities of the speakers that would be difficult for them to bring up modestly themselves. You should be able to get this information in a short interview with each speaker.

In planning the development of your panel, remember these characteristics of a good panel:

1. Interesting. It should not be too repetitious and should include personal references and anecdotes by panel members for human interest.

2. Flexible. It should move easily from one step or one point to another, but it should not do this so abruptly that it fails to allow time for a full discussion of each point.

3. Enthusiastic. Remember to include material that will allow you to communicate yourself with conviction and enthusiasm.

4. Constructive. Be sure that your material is specific and informative and that it is not offensive or abusive.

As in the last assignment, hand in your completed outline form immediately after the panel. Give the instructor's evaluation sheet to him or her in advance, for his or her use during the presentation.

PRACTICE

It is probably best not to rehearse the discussion. You might lose the spontaneity that you will want in the actual presentation. However, do get together for a warm-up session. During the session, the discussion leader can explain (and adjust, if necessary) the time schedule, and the group can discuss the kinds of material to be presented at each step in the discussion. Check to be sure that all members of the panel have enough material to contribute at each step. You may decide to have the group leader call on certain people to present certain ideas or arguments. This is a good way to give reticent speakers a chance to contribute, and to insure the best statement of an important or difficult point. Keep this kind of assigning to a minimum, though, using it only when there is a very good reason. Otherwise your discussion will turn out like a symposium instead of a panel.

When participating in your panel, remember these suggestions:

1. Be both interesting and interested.

2. Contribute to the discussion.

3. Don't monopolize the discussion.

4. Be polite.

5. Avoid gossip and unnecessarily unpleasant matters.

6. Use personal experience, and tell about it with vivid details.

7. Be enthusiastic.

8. Don't change the subject too abruptly.

9. Make a special effort to understand what others mean.

DELIVERY

If you are a member of the panel, be courteous, tactful, and enthusiastic in your delivery. Refer to your notes for facts, names, and quotations, but don't read from them. Keep the tone of the discussion conversational and informal, but talk to the audience, not to the other members of the panel. Although some debate will be necessary and desirable to test solutions, don't spend all your time on debate. Your purpose is not to win your point but to cooperate with others in reaching an acceptable solution to the problem. No one should monopolize the conversation, but each person should speak several times during the discussion. When you have new ideas to contribute, when you have questions to pose, or when you feel a need to clarify or challenge the statements of others—do it.

If you are the leader, be enthusiastic when you introduce the problem and the speakers, so that the discussion gets off to a good start. Show your own positive attitude toward the discussion and the panel. If you feel that something worthwhile is about to be accomplished, so will the panel and the audience. Bring out controversy where it exists, but diplomatically stop or prevent debates that are too personal or will take too long. In a friendly but firm way, you must hold the discussion to the topic and see that there is time to discuss all the solutions properly.

Be impartial—toward ideas, toward members of the panel, and toward members of the audience. However, impartiality should not make you seem uninterested, cold, or remote. Ask for facts, examples, experience, or source when unsupported opinions are offered, and help the audience by using the blackboard when appropriate to list solutions or pertinent facts. Pay close attention to everything that is said, taking notes on your outline so that you can summarize whenever it seems necessary. For instance, you should summarize after a speaker presents a lengthy or vague idea and after each problem-solving step (to show where agreement has been reached and where controversy still exists) as well as present in your final summary the main points that have been considered and the solutions that have been favored. Periodic summaries are essential to help the audience keep track of the discussion and to make them feel that it is accomplishing its purpose. Just be sure that you summarize what actually has been done and not what you think should have been done.

In your warm-up session, keep these characteristics of good panelists in mind:

1. They express themselves well.

2. They are open-minded.

3. They have done many things and also supplemented their firsthand experiences through listening to others tell about their experiences, through reading, and so forth.

4. They have flexible and interesting voices.

5. They are enthusiastic and show an ability to stimulate others.

6. They have a sense of humor.

CRITICISM

Even when your own panel is leading the discussion, you will be doing more listening than speaking. Listen creatively: try to understand what each speaker means as well as what he or she says. At the same time, listen critically, as you would to a persuasive speech. Here are some questions that will help you evaluate the ideas as they are presented:

1. Does the speaker state his or her position clearly?

2. Does he or she have experience to use in support?

3. Does he or she present facts where needed?

4. Does he or she furnish examples?

5. Does he or she use testimony by authorities?

6. Does he or she name his or her sources?

7. Are his or her sources reliable?

8. Does he or she impartially present facts on both sides of a controversy?

9. Does he or she use logic and reason in developing his or her ideas?

No speaker is likely to do all these things in presenting one idea, but he or she should do some of them each time. If he or she does not, ask for supporting material. If the speaker cannot provide it, you are entitled to suspect the validity of his or her opinions.

OUTLINE: USING THE PANEL

I THE PROBLEM

(Show how the problem developed and use examples, statistics, facts, and testimony to establish the size and scope of the problem)

OUTLINE: USING THE PANEL

II CRITERIA FOR SOLUTION

(Show all necessary characteristics of a satisfactory solution)

OUTLINE: USING THE PANEL

III SUGGESTED SOLUTIONS

(List all possible solutions)

OUTLINE: USING THE PANEL

IV DISCUSSION

(List arguments for and against each solution, and test each solution against the criteria)

OUTLINE: USING THE PANEL

V CONCLUSIONS

(Indicate the amount of acceptance for each solution and summarize the major reasons given for accepting or rejecting the solution)

1. All favored this solution:

    Reasons:

2. Most favored this solution:

    Reasons:

OUTLINE: USING THE PANEL

3. Many favored this solution:

Reasons:

4. Few favored this solution:

Reasons:

5. No one favored this solution:

Reasons:

NOTE: To be handed in after the discussion

INSTRUCTOR'S EVALUATION: USING THE PANEL

1. Preparation

A. Understanding of problem
B. Understanding of criteria
C. Preparation of solution
D. Possession of facts
E. Possession of examples
F. Possession of testimony
G. Naming of sources
H. Use of logic and reason

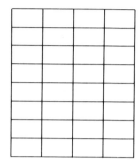

2. Participation

A. Enthusiasm
B. Voice
C. Cooperation
D. Tact
E. Courtesy
F. Clarity of expression
G. Presentation of new ideas
H. Clarification of other ideas
I. Challenging of ideas

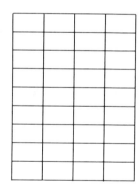

INSTRUCTOR'S EVALUATION: USING THE PANEL

3. Comments

GRADE _____   INSTRUCTOR _____

5
LISTENING

12

LEARNING TO LISTEN

Experts estimate that people learn about eight-five percent of what they know by listening, but that they remember only about twenty percent of what they hear. Obviously, there is a great deal to be gained by improving your listening skills.

The listener must be looked upon as an equal partner in the communication process. Listening is as active as speaking, and in some ways even more difficult. The speaker knows what he or she is going to say, but the listener must interpret the message as it progresses. To do this he or she must understand what is being said, remember what has been said, and project into the future what probably will be said. The listener cannot—as a reader can—go back and review if he or she has missed something or look ahead to see what is coming.

Listening well requires attention, thought, interpretation, and imagination. Listeners must project themselves into the mind of the speaker and attempt to understand not just what the speaker says but what he or she *means*. Inaccuracies in the use of language, changes in the meanings of words from person to person and from context to context—such things can make listening with understanding extremely difficult. The listener must pay attention not only to the words themselves but to the speaker's vocal tones, inflection patterns, and nonverbal symbols such as facial expressions, movements, and gestures. The listener who is alert to signals like these will find it easier to understand the speaker's ideas, and easier to sense the speaker's *feelings* as well.

This may sound like a difficult task, and it is. But it is not impossible, and it is worth the effort. Here are some practical suggestions to help you improve your listening skills.

1. *Adopt a positive attitude.*

Assume that the speaker is an interesting person, someone who is worth knowing and who will present some useful or enjoyable material. As he or she talks, look for clues to his or her personality and for information that really does interest you. Most people are genuinely interesting to a person who listens well.

When I was in college I took a history class from an instructor who was generally considered a very dull lecturer. He sat behind his desk and read his notes in a dull monotone. The other students I knew approached the lectures with the attitude that they would be bored by his dull delivery, and that they would learn nothing. This turned out to be a self-fulfilling prophecy: they *were* bored, and they *did* learn nothing. I, on the other hand, approached the lectures determined to get something from them—perhaps because I found that if I listened carefully I didn't have to read the text. At any rate, I found the lectures to be the best organized I have ever heard, and I thought the examples, details, facts, and language were fascinating. I liked the course better than any other history course I ever took. I learned a great deal about history and particularly the people who made it. My classmates, who apparently listened only to the monotone and nothing else, were amazed at how well I did in the course despite little time spent studying, just by listening well in class.

2. Be responsive.

Ask yourself what the speaker wants from you. He or she probably wants you to be informed, convinced, or entertained. When you understand the response desired, let the speaker know in some appropriate way whether he or she is getting it. Through alert posture you can show that you are listening. A slight nod shows that you understand and the speaker can move on. A puzzled expression shows that you do not fully understand and want the speaker to expand his or her explanations. A tilt of the head or a narrowing of the eyes may show that you are critical of the speaker's opinion and that he or she must present examples and facts to support it. A laugh at the speaker's humor shows you are enjoying the speech, which will spur the speaker on to greater energy and enthusiasm. Don't try to fake a response, but do let a genuine one show so that the speaker knows he or she is not just talking to himself or herself. As any actor can tell you, an apathetic audience makes it almost impossible to give a really good performance. But the give-and-take between a good actor, entertainer, or speaker and a responsive audience can create a truly exciting atmosphere and turn an ordinary experience into a memorable one.

3. *Shut out distractions.*

This is perhaps a difficult suggestion to follow, because even under the best of circumstances your mind is likely to wander off the subject at least two or three times a minute. Thoughts like "I wonder if I remembered to turn off the stove," "This seat is uncomfortable," or "My nose itches" come and go so quickly that the lapse in concentration is hardly recognized. But keep these lapses to a minimum. Don't let noises, other people, or extraneous thoughts create "static" that makes you miss important parts of the message you are trying to receive. Focus your energy and your attention on the speaker and what he or she is saying.

4. *Listen for the speaker's purpose.*

Somewhere near the beginning of the message, the speaker will probably state or imply his or her purpose. Listen for it. Try to understand the basic purpose of the talk so that you will know what the speaker wants you to get out of it.

5. *Look for signals of what is to come.*

Most experienced speakers state their purpose clearly, emphasize their main points, and offer previews of the body of the speech in order to help their listeners follow what they say. For example, in writing this chapter, I stated my purpose at the end of the fourth paragraph, in the sentence "Here are some practical suggestions to help you improve your listening skills." The sentence indicates what I planned to do and how; it alerts you to the fact that the main points of the chapter will be presented in the form of suggestions. To emphasize the suggestions, I numbered them, stated them in parallel grammatical form, and used italics. The italics serve the same purpose visually that vocal emphasis does orally. They show the reader that a new main point is beginning, and he or she knows that the discussion will concern that point until another italic signpost appears. I did not give you a preview of the body of the chapter by saying that there would be eight suggestions in all, or by listing them all before explaining each one in detail, because you are reading and can look back or ahead if you wish. If I were speaking to you, I would probably have done both.

Another clue of what is to come is the organizational pattern of the talk. If a speaker is telling a story, you can expect to hear a series of events in the order that they happened. If the speaker begins with his or her most important point, you can expect to hear a series of points in descending order of importance. If the speaker starts with the easiest concept, you can expect to hear a series of concepts in ascending order of difficulty. If he or she begins with a problem, you can expect to hear about a proposed solution. If he or she begins describing a picture or chart from the left, you can expect him or her to discuss its parts moving from left to right.

259

You will not always be correct in your assumptions of what is to come, but thinking ahead and checking on your assumptions as the speech progresses will help you concentrate and show you the order and coherence in the speaker's message.

6. Look for summaries of what has gone before.

Besides offering clues about what is to come, experienced speakers usually provide summaries or reminders of what has gone before. They do this to be sure that you heard the important points and see how the points are related to each other and to help you remember them. For example, the first main point in a speech on the causes of highway accidents might be stated this way: "The major cause of highway accidents is a failure to obey the laws." Then, when the speaker stated the second main point, he or she might say "A second cause of highway accidents, only slightly less important than the failure to obey laws, is lack of courtesy." This statement does quite a bit more than merely introduce a new point. It includes a reminder of the subject of the talk, an indication of relation between the first two main points, and a restatement of the first main point. You can use summaries and reminders like these to check your understanding and to assist your memory. If the speaker does not provide them, make them up mentally for yourself.

7. Evaluate the supporting materials.

If the situation calls for critical listening, as in persuasion and problem solving, listen carefully for logical explanations, relevant examples, facts, and testimony. If possible, show the speaker through your responses that you want him to furnish these before you accept his opinions as valid. By word or by facial expression, encourage (rather than challenge) him to further explain and support his ideas. He will be delighted if he feels that you are interested and really want to hear more.

8. Look for nonverbal clues.

A speaker's posture, gesture, facial expression, and movement are a vital part of his or her message. Being alert to these nonverbal signals will help you understand how the idea *feels* to the speaker. They also help you evaluate the speaker's sincerity, honesty, conviction, and general integrity, which may be especially important in critical listening.

If you listen well, you will understand better and remember longer the information that others have to offer you. Improving your listening can also help you form closer bonds with other people, because it lets you know them better and because your understanding encourages them to communicate more. And knowing how to listen makes it possible for you to observe and adopt methods of organization, development, and delivery that you can use yourself to aid those who listen to you.

13

IMPROVING YOUR
LISTENING

You will give many speeches during this course, but you will probably listen to at least twenty times more. Thus you have an almost unequaled opportunity to improve your skill at an essential part of the communication process, listening.

On the pages that follow, you will find a sample listening form for each assignment in Chapters 1 through 11. The forms are to guide you in listening to and taking notes on the presentations of your classmates. Prepare as many forms for each assignment as the size of your class requires, collect them in a separate listening notebook, and use them to take notes on the speeches that the other members of the class give throughout the course. Regular, guided practice will make you a better listener, and the notes will be helpful when you try to identify your own strengths and weaknesses and offer constructive criticisms to your classmates.

LISTENING FOR ENJOYMENT

The first few assignments in this book will give you a chance to use listening to get to know the members of your class. Look for information about each person's character and personality in what he or she says and how he or she says it, and also in what he or she doesn't say. Vocal tone, facial expressions, gestures and movements can help you understand how a speaker *feels* about what he or she is saying. Think about the experiences a speaker is relating, the speaker's feelings toward them, and how he or she expresses these feelings. You may have had similar experiences yourself—did they cause similar feelings, and would you express them the same way?

Chapter 1. Introducing Yourself

Speaker 1. Name
Note during the speech:
Personal data

Major   Minor
Hobbies and special interests

Chapter 2. Telling Your Experience for Enjoyment

Speaker 1. Name
Note during the speech:
Experience related

Emotional effect desired

Check after the speech:

	Excellent	Good	Fair	Poor
Giving specific details in descriptions				
Using dialogue to develop characters, emotions				
Suggesting the characters through expressions and gestures				

Chapter 3. Telling Your Experience to Make a Point

Speaker 1. Name
Note during the speech:

Experience related

Emotional effect desired

Point

Check after the speech:

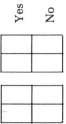

	Yes	No
Did the speaker state the ideas he or she held before the experience?		
Did the speaker give his or her transitional thoughts?		
Did the speaker show the point as a logical outcome of the experience?		
Was the point properly limited?		

LISTENING FOR INFORMATION

In listening for information, you should continue to try to know the speaker as an individual and to be aware of how he or she feels about his or her subject. In addition, listen for the speaker's statement or implication of specific purpose, and for his or her main points. This will help you understand and remember the information the speaker is offering you.

Chapter 4. Giving a Demonstration

Speaker 1. Name

Note during the speech:
   Purpose
   Main points

Check after the speech:

	Excellent	Good	Fair	Poor
Voice				
Enthusiasm				
Posture				
Appearance				
Gestures				
Eye contact				
Movement				

Chapter 5. Using Visual Aids

Speaker 1. Name

Note during the speech:
   Purpose
   Main points

Check after each speech:

Setting up of visual aids				
Handling of visual aids				
Timing of visual aids with speech				
Visibility of visual aids				
Clarity of visual aids				

Chapter 6. Communicating with Anecdotes

Speaker 1. Name

Note during the speech:
  Purpose
  Main points

	Excellent	Good	Fair	Poor
Check after the speech:				
Appropriateness of anecdotes				
Delivery of anecdotes				
Use of direct address (I, you, we)				

Comments (Make additional notes on strengths and weaknesses you observed in the organization, material, and delivery of the speech.)

LISTENING TO PERSUASION

Listening to persuasion requires that you understand the other person—what the person means as well as what he or she says—as does listening for enjoyment. It requires that you see the purpose of the speech and its main points, as does listening for information. In addition, it requires critical evaluation of the supporting materials. See the criticism sections in Chapters 8 and 9 for suggestions on how to do this.

However, don't become too critical too soon. If you are opposed to the speaker's position, give him or her a fair hearing before you begin formulating your own arguments. If the speaker mentions a subject (such as sex, drugs, abortion, or black power) about which you have strong feelings, be careful not to let your feelings blot out the rest of what he or she has to say. Words are merely symbols and, as such, are neither good nor bad in themselves. If you have a strong emotional reaction to a word or an idea, it's because it is important to you personally. Therefore it is even more important than usual for you to listen carefully and understand what's being said.

Chapter 7. Supporting One Point

Speaker 1. Name

Note during the speech:
  Point

	Excellent	Good	Fair	Poor

Check after the speech:
  Amount of material
  Suitability of material
  Sources of material
  Credit for sources
  Use of specific language

Chapter 8. Taking a Side on a Controversial Issue

Speaker 1. Name

Note during the speech:
  Problem
  Solution

Check after the speech:
  Statement of problem
  Statement of solution
  Visualization of results
  Appeal for action
  Use of logic
  Use of valid supporting materials

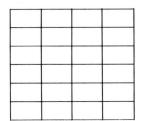

Chapter 9. Calling for Action

Speaker 1. Name

Note during the speech:
  Problem
  Solution

Check after the speech:
  Statement of problem
  Statement of solution
  Visualization of results
  Appeal for action
  Appeals to drives, motives, and so forth
  Use of logic
  Use of valid supporting materials
  Development of favorable speaker image

LISTENING TO SOLVE PROBLEMS

Listening to solve problems requires techniques used in listening to persuasion and, in addition, you must enter into the communication as a speaker as well. To do this you must understand the problem, the criteria for a good solution, and the possible solutions. It is essential that you fairly and open-mindedly consider all solutions. Be prepared to compromise if necessary to reach a solution that will be acceptable to the majority of the group.

Chapter 10.   Using the Symposium

Symposium 1.

Note during the discussion:
  Discussion leader
  Speakers

  Problem
  Proposed solutions
  Best solution

	Yes	No
Check after the discussion:		
Was the problem clearly stated?		
Were the criteria clearly stated?		
Were all possible solutions properly considered?		
Were pertinent examples, statistics, facts, and testimony given?		
Was the solution selected really the best on the basis of the evidence given?		
Briefly explain any "no" answers:		

Chapter 11.   Using the Panel

Panel 1.

Note during the discussion:
  Discussion leader
  Members of panel

  Problem
  Proposed solutions

  Best solution

266

Yes No

Check after the discussion:

Was the problem clearly stated?

Were the criteria clearly stated?

Were all possible solutions properly considered?

Were pertinent examples, statistics, facts,
and testimony given?

Was the solution selected really the best on the basis
of the evidence given?

Briefly explain any "no" answers:

6
IMPROVING ORAL COMMUNICATION

14
ANALYZING YOUR AUDIENCE

The more you know about your audience—its size, the number of men and women in it, their ages, their occupations, their interests—the easier it will be for you to communicate effectively in your own talks. Using the notes you took on the listening forms during the introductory speeches, answer the following questions about your audience.

1. SIZE How many people are there in your audience? This is important because the larger the audience, the more energy you must expend in order to project your voice, personality, and enthusiasm to them. Also, you will generally get larger reactions—especially to humor—from larger audiences.

NUMBER IN AUDIENCE _____

2. SEX How many men and women are there in your audience? This should not govern the topics you select, but it should affect the way you treat the topics. If your audience consists of both men and women, your introductions must capture the attention of both sexes, and your examples and language must be suitable to both. A talk about a handball game, for instance, could be enjoyable for women as well as for men, but the speaker might have to describe the game and perhaps include reminders about its rules.

NUMBER OF MEN _____ NUMBER OF WOMEN_____

3. AGE About how old is your audience, on the average? What is

the approximate age of the youngest and the oldest members of the class? People's interests and responsibilities differ according to their ages and so do their attitudes toward such matters as education, dating, employment, marriage, child raising, security, and retirement. In planning your speeches, show that you understand the concerns of *all* the members of your audience.

AVERAGE AGE_____ AGE RANGE: FROM _____ TO_____

4. OCCUPATION   Most people in your audience are probably full-time students. Are there exceptions? What occupations do the members of the class plan to enter after they have completed their education? What experiences have you had that are relevant, directly or indirectly, to the fields they have chosen?

OCCUPATION OF MOST_____

OTHER OCCUPATIONS_____

_____

_____

5. COMMON INTERESTS   With a varied audience like the one you probably have, common interests can be difficult to determine. However, the information you have noted above about age, sex, and occupation can tell you quite a bit, especially if you draw on conversations you have had with parents, relatives, and friends as well as on your own experience. The notes you took on the introductory speeches of your classmates should suggest some additional common interests. The list of motives given on page 177 might also be helpful. What motives can you assume most members of your audience share? Refer to all these interests and motives when selecting topics for your speeches, and when selecting the material and language to develop your ideas.

COMMON INTERESTS (from introductory speeches):

_____

_____

_____

_____

_____

_____

_____

_____

_____

_____

_____

_____

_____

_____

_____

   COMMON INTERESTS AND MOTIVES (assumed on the basis of age, sex, and occupation, and drawn from motives listed in Chapter 9):

_____

_____

_____

_____

_____

_____

_____

_____

_____

_____

   Whenever you communicate with anyone—whether in a prepared speech, a group discussion, or an informal conversation—make the same kind of analysis you have made here, and adjust your purpose and your material accordingly. Real communication is not just talking; it is talking _to_ someone. You must show that someone, whether he or she is your whole audience or only a small part of it, that you are aware of him or her as an individual and that you are concerned about his or her interests, ideas, and feelings. Everyone you speak to should feel that he or she is important to you. If you really feel this way, it will show in what you say and how you say it; if you do not, that will show too. You can probably tell when a speaker is unsure (or wrong) about the interests of an audience that you are part of, or when he or she is insincere or patronizing. So, when you are the speaker, learn as much as you can about your listeners in advance, and make a serious effort to understand their point of view.

15

UNDERSTANDING THE PROCESS OF ORAL COMMUNICATION

There may be times in your life when professional, service, or social organizations that you belong to will ask you to make a speech reporting on the progress of your group, advocating or opposing some proposition, or explaining some procedure. Your advancement in these organizations may depend on your ability to do this effectively. The material in this book has been designed partly to give you principles and practice that will prepare you for these occasions.

But preparing you for the few occasions you may have for platform speaking is not the sole aim of this book. Its major aim is to make you more effective in all your oral communication. Oral communication is your most valuable tool. It is a tool for pleasure, for information, for persuasion, and for problem solving. In our society, it will not only determine your ability to reach objective goals but affect your happiness and your mental health as well.

In order to improve communication, you must first understand what it is. Briefly stated, communication is the act of sending ideas and feelings in such a way that the receiver can re-create those ideas and feelings for himself or herself. This implies three essentials: the sender, the message, and the receiver.

The sender begins the process by making a decision to communicate. He or she then mentally sorts through all the symbols at his or her command (words, gestures, facial expressions, vocal tones, and so forth) and selects the ones that will best communicate the intended meaning. He or she organizes these symbols into a reasonable pattern, which forms the message, and transmits them to the receiver. The receiver must call upon his or her own previous experience with these symbols in order to determine their meaning and then re-create the ideas and feelings for himself or herself.

One of the most common errors made in thinking about communication is to assume that listening or receiving the message is a passive act. It is as active, mentally and emotionally, as sending the message.

The process of communication may be compared to coding and decoding a message. When you were a child, you may have played games in which you invented secret codes for sending messages to your friends. Perhaps you assigned numbers to the letters of the alphabet and wrote out a message in numbers instead of letters so that your friends had to decode in order to reconstruct the message. The process of communication is exactly the same except that, because the symbols we use are more easily recognized, we code and decode the messages so rapidly that we hardly realize what we are doing.

On the surface the process seems simple, but it is actually extremely complex and difficult—so difficult, in fact, that many great writers in literature, psychology, and communication have suggested that real communication is impossible.

Why is it so difficult? If we know what we mean, and we send symbols that our receiver can recognize, why can't he or she recreate precisely the same message that we send? There are many places where communication can break down, and successful communication requires that we be aware of the problems and take steps to prevent them.

To begin with, the sender may make a mistake. One of the most common is for senders to assume because they know what they mean that the receiver will also know what they mean. This usually leads to an inadequate message. In these cases the sender often "cops out" by saying "You know?" "Get what I mean?" or "I can't say it, but you know what I mean." The receiver then is forced to fill in the details from his or her own experience, which may be so different from the sender's that the message he or she recreates is very different from the one the sender thought he or she sent.

There are many other breakdowns in communication that may originate with senders. They may not decide carefully what the purpose of their message is. They may not organize it in such a way that it is coherent. Or they may use words and gestures that have more than one meaning. If the meaning the speaker intends is not made clear, the symbols are left ambiguous, and the receiver can select the wrong one in decoding the message.

Since the receiver is an equal partner in the communication process, we must also consider problems that can occur in the decoding of the message. If receivers are bored or preoccupied, they may simply not receive all of the message. They may assume that they know what the sender is going to say and, instead of listening, begin planning what they will say when their turn comes. This is especially likely to happen when receivers are opposed to the sender's position. They begin preparing their rebuttal to the sender's arguments before they really know what those arguments are; even when they try to listen, they tend to judge and evaluate the message instead of re-creating it. A third possibility is that the receivers, instead of trying to understand what the sender means, call entirely upon their own experience with the symbols used, creating a new message of their own instead of re-creating the one the sender is trying to transmit.

The problems of planning, organizing, and delivering a message are covered in Parts 1 through 4, but there are two causes of communication breakdowns that we should consider in more detail at this point.

One of these is the tendency to judge or evaluate people's thoughts and feelings instead of trying to understand them. Carl Rogers, a leading thinker on modern psychology and semantics, describes this as "the greatest barrier to mutual interpersonal communication."*

Here is a familiar example. You ask your parents for additional spending money. They reply that you don't need it because you're irresponsible in handling the money you have. You say "That isn't true!" and the next thing you know someone is in tears. This example involves not only evaluation instead of understanding but an additional factor—emotion. The two (emotion and hasty evaluation) often go together, and when they do, real communication is almost sure to be impossible.

What is the solution? Rogers says it is to listen with understanding, to try to see the expressed idea from the other person's point of view and to understand how the idea feels to *him*. Understand how *he* feels about money, or his children, or himself, or whatever is being discussed. The first step in changing a person's behavior is understanding *with* him, not *about* him.

To test the quality of your understanding, Rogers suggests this laboratory experiment. The next time you get in an argument with a parent, a friend, or an acquaintance, stop the argument and institute this rule. Each person can speak for himself only after he has expressed the point of view of the previous speaker—and to that speaker's satisfaction. You'll find this will slow the argument down! You'll also find the emotion going out of the situation, and with it the differences between the speakers. The few differences that remain will be rational—the kind that can be dealt with easily.

Another cause of communication breakdowns, closely related to the previous one, is the tendency to defend the ego by defending what one has said. As soon as there is a disagreement, we feel that we are in competition and must win at all costs. Sometimes the cost is the loss of a friend.

*Carl R. Rogers, "Communication: Its Blocking and Its Facilitation," *Etc.*, Winter, 1952. This paper was originally presented at Northwestern University's Centennial Conference on Communications, October 11, 1951.

I remember reading a newspaper filler that said, "You can't win an argument." My first reaction was, "What does he mean you can't win an argument? Of course you can win an argument. I've won lots of arguments." (You see, I was evaluating the author's statement.) But while thinking about arguments that I have participated in, I began to understand the statement. In arguments that I remembered losing, I knew I had "lost," but I hesitated to admit to myself that I had been wrong. In arguments that I seemed to have won, my opponent probably was equally hesitant to admit that he was wrong.

We seldom admit that we have really lost an argument. We may admit that the other person can talk louder or longer, that he is better read on the subject, or even that he has more facts at his disposal, but we often think, "I'll do some more research on the subject, and next time I'll show him!"

Of course, you may be able to present such a strong case that you humiliate your opponent into accepting your position. But you may lose a friend, and if you lose a friend you haven't really won anything.

I have a friend who is always getting into arguments. Once into one, he will never admit that he might be wrong, no matter what the evidence is on the opposing side.

One evening he and his wife came to visit my wife and me. On the way they had begun arguing about the meaning of a word. When they arrived, before my friend even said hello he came up to me and said, "You're an English teacher—you ought to know this!" and asked me to settle the argument by picking one of the definitions.

I didn't really want to be in that position, but there seemed to be no way out except to select a definition and hope for the best. Unfortunately, the definition I picked was his wife's definition, and so he insisted that I was wrong. (Now that I disagreed with him, I was no longer an authority.)

I decided not to argue the point. I simply said that I use the word that way and suggested that he look it up in the dictionary. He did, and the dictionary agreed with his wife and me. So he insisted that the dictionary was wrong.

I still didn't argue with him. I pointed out that my dictionary was abridged and suggested that he go to the library the next day and look into an unabridged dictionary. Perhaps he would find what he was looking for there.

After that we forgot about the word and settled down to a pleasant, sociable evening. The strategy I used to prevent an argument that could have ruined the evening was partly to avoid humiliating my opponent, because that would have made it impossible for him to accept my suggestions.

The other part of the strategy was to avoid contradicting directly. I didn't say "I think you're wrong." Whenever you do that you can expect the other person to become rigid in defense of what he has said. What you should remember is that as he sees the situation he is right. So what you say to him is, "You're right as far as you go, but you haven't seen all the facts." None of us wants to admit that we are wrong, but most of us don't mind admitting that we don't know everything.

I used this strategy more pointedly with the same friend in another situation, during a visit to his home. He was working on a speech that he planned to deliver the following day. He showed me his manuscript and asked me to help him with the speech.

The speech was on a very controversial topic—one highly charged with emotion. As I read through the speech, I was appalled. There were no facts and no logic—only emotional appeals. I didn't know exactly what to do. If I told him the speech was no good he would surely become angry, and then I would be unable to help him. My first thought was to take the coward's way out and say "Yeah, Jim, it's a great speech! Go ahead and deliver it just that way." If he should get booed off the stage (and I considered that a very real possibility), I could always say, "You had a great speech but a lousy audience."

I couldn't bring myself to do that. After all, he was a friend of mine, and he had asked my help on something that I was qualified to help him with. But how? I spent several minutes looking at the manuscript, supposedly studying it but actually trying frantically to find the right approach to the problem.

Then I remembered: As the other person sees the situation, he is probably right. "That must be it," I thought, "after all, he's not stupid. Why did he write his speech this way?"

When I thought I had it figured out, I put down the manuscript and said, "Yeah, Jim, this is a great speech. It's full of powerful emotional appeals. The people in your audience who agree with you are going to swell up with pride when they hear this speech!"

"That's what I thought," he smiled back proudly. I knew I was on the right track.

So I added, "But you've got to remember that everyone in your audience won't agree with you. Basically there are three kinds of people in your audience: those who agree with you and will agree with you no matter what you say, those who disagree with you and will disagree with you no matter what you say, and those who are undecided. There's no point worrying much about the first two groups, because what you say to them won't make much difference anyway. The group you really want to reach is the undecideds. And if you want to persuade them, you've got to give them logic and facts, not just emotional appeals."

"I hadn't thought about it that way," he said. Then we set about the job of revising his speech—he with a great deal of enthusiasm and I with a sigh of relief.

To summarize, you will improve your ability to send and to receive messages—that is, to communicate—if you keep the following things in mind:

1. One of the major causes of communication breakdowns is the tendency to evaluate the statements of others.

2. Another important cause of communication breakdowns is the tendency to defend one's ego by defending what one has said.

3. When speaking, think of the *total effect* of your communication (vocal tone, gestures, expressions, and so forth), not just the words used.

4. When listening, try to understand what the speaker *means*, not just what he or she says.

5. Since some misunderstandings are inevitable, try to create an atmosphere in which people feel free to ask questions.

6. Don't directly contradict or disprove. Contradict or disprove indirectly, preserving the other person's ego in the process.

7. Where individuals disagree, ask each to state the other's position to the satisfaction of the other. Try this even when you are one of the people involved.

8. Remember, *as the other person sees the situation* he or she is probably right.

9. Take every honest opportunity to make the other person feel better or more important.

10. Be honest and open in your communication.

Communication is a cooperative effort. The sender and the receiver must share the responsibility. Each must demonstrate clearly that he cares about the other and is really eager to cooperate in the act of communication.

In communication (as in life) you must give in order to receive. What you can receive in enjoyment, information, and influence is in direct proportion to what you are willing to give the other person. If you enter wholeheartedly into the act of communication, the rewards are great.

QUESTIONS FOR DISCUSSION

1. How do we perceive objects and events? Why is our perception always different from that of any other person?

2. How do we learn words and other symbols? How can this process lead to communication barriers?

3. Why are words like *administration, politician, democracy, communism, freedom,* and *religion* especially difficult to interpret? Can you add some words to the list?

4. Sometimes instead of asking of a word, "What does *it* mean?" it is more useful to ask of a person, "What do *you* mean?" Why might this be the case?

5. What are some communication problems that might arise from the following?

   A speaker who seems concerned only with himself.
   A speaker who seems concerned only with her message.

A listener who seems concerned only with himself.
An unenthusiastic speaker.
An overly enthusiastic speaker.
Directly disagreeing by saying, "I think you're wrong."
A speaker who keeps saying "You know what I mean?" instead of giving specific details.

6. During the next twenty-four hours, look for misunderstandings that indicate communication breakdowns in your own conversations and in conversations that you can observe. Report briefly on some of these and their probable causes.

16

EXAMINING THE KINDS OF COMMUNICATION

If there are others present, you cannot choose not to communicate. That's one option that is not open to you. You may, of course, choose not to *talk,* but you will still communicate by:

Your position in relation to others

Your facial expressions

Your eyes

Your posture

Your gestures

Your clothing

Your handling of objects around you

Your handling of the space around you

Others may misread the signals:

Your shyness may be interpreted as conceit.

Your loneliness may be interpreted as aloofness.

Your nervousness may be interpreted as impatience.

Your headache may be interpreted as disapproval.

Your eye strain may be interpreted as anger.

But you will communicate something! So it is better to enter purposefully into the act of communication in order to make your communication as clear and unambiguous as possible. The brief analysis of communication given in Chapter 15 shows something of the complexity of the process. At best, communication is always somewhat ambiguous. It is necessary for us to make every effort to be as clear and specific as possible to prevent misunderstandings.

When you make the decision to communicate, there are five kinds of communication available to you: (1) intrapersonal, (2) interpersonal, (3) small-group, (4) public, and (5) media communication.

INTRAPERSONAL

In this kind of communication the individual communicates with himself or herself. All of us spend a great deal of time in dialogues with ourselves. Some of the time we are consciously explaining and analyzing things to clarify them for ourselves or to prepare for some future communication. On these occasions the dialogue is frequently clear. We ask questions, give answers, and examine related issues and points almost as if we were two people talking to each other. We talk to ourselves, and we answer ourselves.

At other times our dialogues are subconscious interactions between our present perceptions and our previously developed concepts, ideals, and principles. It is in these dialogues that what we call *self* is formed.

At the beginning of each activity in this book you are called upon to engage in intrapersonal dialogues with yourself. In Part 1 you are asked to examine yourself and your experiences; in Part 2 you are asked to examine your knowledge; in Part 3 you are asked to examine your convictions; and in Part 4 you are asked to examine your problems.

INTERPERSONAL

Communication between two people is referred to as interpersonal or "dyadic" communication. This is characterized by an *interaction* in which both people are aware of sending and receiving messages. The sending and receiving occur almost simultaneously, so it is often difficult to determine when a person is sending and when he or she is receiving a message. For example, a man who is talking is clearly sending a message.

But as he talks he continually searches the reactions of his listener—the facial expressions, gestures, or sounds that indicate the degree of attention, understanding, and acceptance of his message. Furthermore, in a process called feedback, he may adjust his message on the basis of these responses. Thus, if the listener looks confused, he may include additional explanation of his material; if the listener seems to disapprove of the message, the speaker may add further material in support of his position. And as the listener's reactions—attention, understanding, approval— alter, he too alters the message he is sending by nonverbal means—that is, his facial expressions, gestures, and sounds. It is this constant reciprocal interaction in which both parties take turns as speaker and listener that is the major characteristic of interpersonal communication.

In interpersonal communication we receive most of our information about ourselves, other people, and the world. In these encounters the unconscious values that are a part of our internal dialogues with ourselves are formed. The amount and value of the information we receive may be governed by the degree to which we are willing to enter into the act of interpersonal communication—particularly the degree to which we are willing to share information about ourselves (self-revelation) and the degree to which we are really willing to *interact* and allow the communication of the other person to affect our thoughts and behavior. Too often we are anxious only to impose our ideas on the other person, and we are unwilling or unable to accept or understand what he or she is saying. To understand the ideas of another person, you must try to see these ideas from that person's point of view—that is, as if they were your own. Thus, your first responsibility is to understand how the other person sees it. To disagree with others is not to say that they are wrong and you right, but that you want them to see the expressed ideas from *another*—your—point of view (this concept is discussed in greater depth in Chapter 15).

This kind of interaction and understanding requires a great deal of energy and flexibility. It requires that you be sensitive to yourself and others, and that you respect yourself as well as others. And it also requires that during the act of interpersonal communication you constantly add to, delete, and reshape your previously held concepts, ideals, and principles.

While there are no organized interpersonal activities presented in this book, you will have the opportunity to practice some of the principles of interpersonal communication. The assignments in Part 1 are somewhat interpersonal in nature in that they emphasize the person (you and your experiences) rather than the task (teaching, persuading, or solving problems). In addition, informal exchanges (both in and out of class) with other class members will frequently be of the interpersonal variety.

As you engage in these exchanges, be analytical of your behavior. Are you really committed to interacting with others? Are you sensitive to your own feelings and their probable causes? Are you capable of seeing ideas from the viewpoints of others? Are you willing to alter and reshape your ideas as you receive new information?

SMALL-GROUP

Small-group communication involves the same principles of inter-action, sensitivity, and understanding as interpersonal communication does. The most obvious difference between dyadic communication and small-group communication is in the number of people involved, which may be three to perhaps twenty. It is important that the group be small enough to allow and encourage all its members to share more or less equally in both the sending and receiving of messages.

Many of our most important and enjoyable hours are spent in com-munication with various small groups: family groups, social groups, therapy groups, learning groups, and work groups. For a group to be most effective, it is important that it have an objective that will hold it together, and that all members of the group be aware of that objective and be willing to cooperate in achieving it. The objective of a social group may be to have a good time together; of a therapy group, self-understanding; and of learning and work groups, the designated goals. These objectives may overlap, of course; for example, a social group may take on a project and, to that extent, become a work group.

Since social groups and therapy groups are generally people-oriented and work groups task-oriented, agendas for such groups should vary accordingly. A social group or a therapy group should have a flexible agenda responsive to the needs and interests of the people involved. A work group should have a tighter agenda that generally involves the following steps, which are discussed at greater length in Chapters 10 and 11:

1. Defining the problem.

2. Establishing requirements of a suitable solution.

3. Offering all possible solutions.

4. Testing each solution through discussion and debate.

5. Selecting the best solution.

But whether the group is person-oriented or task-oriented, its mem-bers should accept the responsibility of contributing to the discussion and encouraging the participation of others through the supportive behavior previously described.

The amount of information to be derived from a group depends on two factors: the backgrounds of the people involved, and their willingness to share information about themselves through interaction with the group. The greater the range in age, experience, and background of the participants, the more information potentially available to the group. One of the benefits to be derived from communication experiences is the opportunity to get to know people different from yourself. For most of our relationships, we tend to select people who are similar to us. This may make for good relationships—because we have a lot in common—but it may also rob us of the enrichment that comes from knowing and understanding people who have different experiences, concepts, and attitudes.

The group discussion activities in this book are of the work-group type. The task of the group is to define and solve problems. However, in panel discussion and forum activities it may often be a good idea to ask yourself the questions listed at the end of the section on interpersonal communication.

PUBLIC

In public communication, or public speaking, one person speaks to many people. Like dyadic and small-group communication, it involves a face-to-face situation and some interaction between the participants. But the interaction is less balanced because one person (the speaker) does most—or all—of the talking, while the group (the audience) does most—or all—of the listening. It is less individually oriented in two ways: Unlike the case in dyadic and small-group communication the speaker must prepare his or her message with the needs and interests of the group, rather than the individual, in mind; and the members of the audience do not have the opportunity to express themselves as individuals to the degree they can in the above-mentioned forms of communication. Public communication is also less spontaneous because the message is generally prepared in advance. Speakers may adjust and adapt their message on the basis of the feedback they get, but not usually to the same degree as in the other forms, and so it is important that they carefully analyze their audience before preparing the message if it is not to be inappropriate (see Chapter 14). This kind of communication is also less balanced in terms of information sharing, because the speaker can give much more information than he or she can receive.

The emphasis in this book is, of course, on public communication. The speeches to inform (Chapters 4, 5, and 6) and the speeches to persuade (Chapters 7, 8, and 9) are the most common types of public speeches. In addition, a group discussion—whether it is a symposium (Chapter 10) or a panel (Chapter 11)—becomes public communication when it is presented for an audience.

MEDIA

In media communication the participants are no longer face-to-face and interacting directly. The message is prepared by the sender and presented to the receiver through an impersonal agency. The most common of these are books, newspapers, magazines, radio, and television. Because the communicator does not have an opportunity to observe reactions to his or her message (feedback being either nonexistent or delayed), it is essential that he or she carefully analyze the nature of his or her intended receiver in advance.

Since the activities in this book focus on speaking and listening rather than reading and writing, you probably will have little or no opportunity to work with mediated communication unless you have the opportunity to broadcast your speeches over television or radio. However, I am communicating with you through a printed medium (this book). As I write this, I visualize you as being like the students I am currently teaching at De Anza College. The effectiveness of my communication may depend on the accuracy of that inference (see the next chapter for a further discussion of inferences).

Communicating face-to-face on an individual level is the most effective way of communicating, but public and media communication are expedient means of disseminating information to large numbers of people, and group discussion is an excellent means of solving problems.

17

GETTING THE FACTS STRAIGHT

A friend of mine and I were discussing a young woman of our acquaintance when my friend startled me with the following assertion. "A guy I know said she was willing to go to bed with him, so I know for a fact she's willing to go to bed with anyone!"

I don't believe that you have to question every inference (opinion) you make or hear, but, in this case, some questioning seemed warranted. So I said, "Wait a minute! You don't know anything *for a fact* except that he *said* she was willing. It is, of course, possible that he was not being completely honest. However, assuming that he was being honest, the only facts would seem to be that (1) he *thought* she was willing, and (2) she *didn't* do it. We are not given the *facts* that led him to his opinion. Given the same facts, we might come up with a different opinion. But even if he is correct in his first assumption, it does not warrant the second assumption that 'she's willing to go to bed with anyone'!"

It is important to clear thinking that we be able to differentiate between fact and inference and judgment. Otherwise, we may pile inference upon inference (as my friend did) and come to widely different (and perhaps illogical) conclusions.

For example, what are the *facts* in the following accounts of the same hypothetical event? (1) "I see a woman with a large shopping bag. She is a housewife doing her shopping. She is probably a good wife and mother." (2) "I see a woman with a large shopping bag. Shoplifters use large shopping bags. She is a shoplifter. She is here to steal. If I don't watch her carefully, she'll steal me blind!" With the exception of the observation of the "shopping bag," the statements are all highly inferential and judgmental. This chapter will examine the differences between facts, inferences, and judgments.

FACTS

A fact may be defined as a statement that can be verified and that is, as far as possible, independent of personal opinion. A fact is *objective* in that it depends on universal standards; an opinion is *subjective* in that it depends on personal standards. "I am 5 feet, 11 inches tall" is a fact; you can verify it by measurement. "I am tall" is an opinion: it depends on personal standards; some people say that is medium in height. Here are some other factual statements:

The water was forty-percent saturated with filterable solids.

De Anza College is located in Cupertino, California.

John was born on February 13, 1944.

Two plus two equal four.

Bill is wearing brown shoes.

Jane weighs 118 pounds.

His debts include a $33,000 mortgage on his home.

These statements are verifiable. (It would be useful to consider how you would go about verifying each, and learning how the verification is based on an objective standard.)

It is important to remember that a factual statement is not necessarily true (but it *is* verifiable). It may be false by accident. A friend said, "There are three houses on your block." Actually, if you were to count (verify the statement), you would find that there are five. Two more have been built recently. Often facts are subject to change by *time*. That is why it is important to get *recent* facts, either by observation or by research. That's why the publication date of research sources often becomes important in both written and oral communication.

It is also possible that facts may be false by design. Demagogues and con artists in particular prey upon the unsuspecting by misrepresenting and distorting facts. By again, *facts are verifiable*. You may ask the source of the information and check it yourself. You may also want to check the source by going to other sources.

It is well to verify facts for yourself where important decisions are to be made. However, if we accepted as facts only those statements that we verified personally, ours would be a very limited existence. We accept as facts many statements coming from books, newspapers, friends, teachers, lawyers, and so on because there are many—such as statements about other times and places—that we cannot verify for ourselves. We frequently accept these "on faith" and without question. But, again, if important decisions are to be made, we may have to question the authority of the person making the statements and his or her supporting evidence.

We should also be aware that even an individual's true facts may be distorted by his or her past experiences and present motivations. Two of my students, for example, gave very different factual accounts of a political demonstration in San Jose. One of the students was himself a demonstrator, and his facts tended to support the position of the demonstrators; the other was a policeman, and his facts tended to support the position of the police. We all tend to do this; that is, we form an opinion and then select facts to support it. In decision making, it is valuable to examine the facts supporting opposing opinions as well.

INFERENCES

An inference is what we have previously described as an opinion. It is not a "sure thing." It is a guess based on fact. Sometimes our inferences are based on many facts, sometimes on a few. It is important to remember, when we infer something, that there are usually other possibilities. For example: I saw a man riding a bicycle. (I inferred that it was a man; it might have been a woman dressed as a man.) It was his bicycle. (It may have been borrowed or stolen.) He was riding to work. (It was 7:45 A.M., he was wearing a suit and carrying a briefcase, but he may have been riding home or to visit a friend.)

An inference is a probability. Whether it is of high or low probability depends on the number and kinds of facts gathered in support. "The sun will rise in the morning" is an inference. It is of course possible that the sun will explode or that the earth will cease to move during the night, but the sun has risen every morning for millions of years, so this is a high-probability inference. "The city bus will be on time in the morning" is of lower probability—especially if it has been late two out of the last five days.

It is necessary for us to make inferences and act on them: "It is raining outside (fact), so we will have to cancel our picnic (inference)." "My husband usually comes home about 5:00 o'clock and wants his dinner at 6:00 o'clock (fact), so I need to have his dinner ready at 6:00 o'clock tonight (inference)." "A car is crossing into my lane (fact), so I ought to slow my car (inference)."

What we call natural laws are not "natural" and they are not "laws." They are inferences made by scientists about the nature of reality. On the basis of facts gathered (research), a scientist forms inferences. Additional research may uncover new facts that will lead to new inferences. For example, when I studied chemistry, I learned that an atom was the smallest particle of matter that could not be separated. Shortly after that the atom was split. That new fact ushered in the "atomic age." Scientific "facts" are based on agreement by the most learned individuals in our society, and so they may be treated as facts. But it is important to remember (as any scientist will tell you) that they are subject to change.

A great problem in communication is that we tend to assume that facts are easily differentiated from inferences. That is not always the case. Sometimes in reporting facts we unconsciously include inferences. A friend said to me, "I see you bought a new shirt."

Although this might seem to be a factual statement based on his observation, the statement reflects two inferences—both wrong. I did not buy the shirt (it was a gift), and it was not new (I simply had not worn it in years). The fact was that he saw me wearing a shirt he had never seen. Watch for hidden inferences in your statements and those of others.

JUDGMENTS

A judgment is like an inference; it expresses an opinion, but it is even more subjective since it also expresses approval or disapproval. In judgments we say a great deal about ourselves. If I say "She is a pretty girl," "He is a nice boy," "You are a good student," I am saying in effect: "I have certain criteria or expectations concerning 'pretty,' 'nice,' and 'good,' and the person I am discussing lives up to my expectations." Another person, with different criteria, might feel differently. In evaluating a judgment, it is necessary to ask not only for the facts but also the criteria on which the judgment was based.

In discussing a mutual acquaintance, you might say to me, "He is conceited." That is not a fact. If I question you, I may find that the fact is he fails to stop and talk to you when he passes you on campus. Even our being in agreement—that is, I also think him conceited, and for the same reason—would not make it a fact. Perhaps he is shy; perhaps he thinks we are the conceited ones because we do not stop to talk to him.

In his book Language in Thought and Action, S. I. Hayakawa gives this analysis of fact, inference and judgment:

> Many people regard statements such as the following as statements of "fact." "Jack lied to us," "Jerry is a thief," "Tommy is clever." As ordinarily employed, however, the word "lied" involves first an inference (that Jack knew otherwise and deliberately misstated the facts) and second a judgment (that the speaker disapproves of what he inferred that Jack did). In the other two instances, we may substitute such expressions as "Jerry was convicted of theft and served two years at Waupun," and "Tommy plays the violin, leads his class at school, and is captain of the debating team." After all, to say of a man that he is a "thief" is to say in effect, "He has stolen and will steal again"—which is more of a prediction than a report. Even to say, "He has stolen" is to make an inference (and simultaneously to pass a judgment) on an act about which there may be differences of opinion among those who have examined the evidence upon which the conviction was obtained. But

to say that he was "convicted of theft" is to make a statement capable of being agreed upon through verification in court and prison records.*

It is not suggested that we question every inference that we make, but simply that we be alive to other possibilities by being aware of our inferences, and that when the situation calls for critical appraisal—as in persuasion (Part 3 of this text) and problem solving (Part 4)—we examine the other possibilities and facts before making decisions.

At the conclusion of his book *Communications: The Transfer of Meaning*, Don Fabun† offers this helpful little "catechism" to use when you hear (or read) something:

1. WHO said so? (Don't accept "they" or "company official" or "someone close to the_____.")

2. WHAT did he say? (What someone says he "thinks" someone else said is probably wrong; forget it.)

3. What did he MEAN? (If you are talking to someone directly, asking some questions may help. If he's not around, then possibly what he meant cannot be established; but in asking the question, you can at least make it clear to yourself that he may not mean what you think he does.)

4. HOW does he know? (Is he an expert? Was he there? What are his sources of information?)

As a speaker, you will help to keep the facts straight if you will do the following:

1. Discuss people, things, and facts with sufficient explanations and examples to clarify your meaning (see Chapter 7), but avoid boring your listener with obvious padding.

2. Differentiate clearly between facts (verifiable reports) and opinions (inferences). Introduce inferences with phrases like: "I think we may infer . . ."; "From these facts I conclude . . ."; "It seems reasonable to assume . . ."; "It is my opinion . . . ," and so on.

3. Quote what has been said (or written), giving *in the text of your speech* the sources. Quotations should be introduced in the following manner: "In this book *Communications: The Transfer of Meaning.* Don Fabun wrote . . ."; "On the C.B.S. news last Tuesday, Walter Cronkite reported . . ."; "In preparation for this speech, I interviewed our student body president, who told me . . ."; and so forth.

4. Where they are appropriate, use statistics. Gather them by personal observation (you may conduct your own polls, for example) or by research. When you are researching, gather the most recent facts possible. Remember, facts are subject to change in time. For clarity and emphasis in oral communication, present statistics in round numbers (three out of five, 95 percent, and so on). Present large, complex numbers *visually* on graphs and charts.

5. When you present judgments, be sure to give your criteria for the

---

*S. I. Hayakawa, "Reports, Inferences, Judgments," *Language in Thought and Action*, 3d ed. (New York: Harcourt Brace Jovanovich, Inc., 1972), pp. 34–48.
†Don Fabun, *Communications: The Transfer of Meaning* (Beverly Hills, California: The Glencoe Press, 1968), p. 47.

judgment. If you say "This is a *bad* law," point out the criteria for a good one and show how this law does not meet them. If you say "He is a *good* administrator," give your criteria for a good administrator and point out how he meets them. If you say "This is a *beautiful* painting," you need to discuss your criteria for beauty in relationship to this painting.

It is not always easy—or even possible—to clearly differentiate between facts, inferences, and judgments. But it is important to make every effort when important decisions are to be made. Keeping the facts straight is essential to clear thinking and rational behavior.

18
CONTROLLING
STAGE FRIGHT

As a teacher of speech and drama, I find that the one question beginning students ask most often is, "How can I get rid of stage fright?" (This is often called "speech fright" or "speaking anxiety.") As a performer (I have done a considerable amount of singing and acting as well as speaking), I find that one question asked most often by people from the audience is, "How can you be so relaxed and calm in front of an audience? Aren't you nervous at all?" Both questions, it seems to me, are based on a misunderstanding of the nature and value of stage fright.

In answer to the second question, I have to point out that I'm *not* "so relaxed and calm." I always have a case of stage fright—butterflies in my stomach *before* a performance and sweaty palms *during* a performance. Sometimes my knees shake and my mouth gets dry. When I am in a play, I always hope that I won't have to handle a cup and saucer during the first few minutes I'm on stage, because I know I'll be shaking enough to make the cup rattle in the saucer. The audience can't see the shaking but they can hear the rattling. I always experience some nervousness when I face an audience, even at the lectures I give daily in my college classes. If other people are unaware of my nervousness, it's because I have learned to control it and use it.

All the performers I have worked with in acting, singing, and speaking have also experienced this nervousness before and during a performance. One of the axioms in show business is, "If you ever get over being nervous about a performance, you're finished." Even established stars get stage fright, sometimes—surprisingly enough—to a greater degree than those of us who have less experience. The bigger their names, the more they feel they must produce to satisfy their audiences and the more frightened they become. One of the greatest operatic tenors of all times, Enrico Caruso, was so nervous before his performances that he always prayed for divine assistance. And I remember a very famous concert pianist who became so nervous before every concert that he would insist he was ill and beg his manager to cancel the performance. What the manager did was simply wait until time for the concert to begin and gently push the pianist onto the stage. Once there, he would give an electrifying performance. The audience had no way of knowing the terrible fears he had experienced.

Once I did a play without stage fright. It was the second time I had played the part, and we had a long rehearsal period. I got bored with the part and the play, and I became overconfident. I remember standing backstage before one of the performances with an empty, dull feeling instead of an exciting, keyed-up, "nervous" one. It was then that I realized that "performance nerves" are part of the fun. Stage fright pulls you out of your everyday routine, sharpens your senses, and makes you alert and sensitive to what goes on around you. It reminds you that you're really alive.

I tried very hard to get nervous before the rest of the performances of that play. I imagined every horrible thing that could possibly happen. I might forget my lines; my costume might fall off; the scenery might fall over on me; other people might forget lines or entrances and leave me stranded alone on the stage. Try as I might, I could not get nervous. I gave probably the worst performance of my life. I still have the newspaper reviews to prove it.

So don't try to get rid of stage fright. Learn to control it and use it. In a fear situation, the organs of your body react. The adrenalin glands pump adrenalin into the muscles to increase their strength and speed up reaction. The heart beats faster and sends more blood and oxygen to the muscles, the brain, and the central nervous system. The liver releases greater quantities of sugar, and the pancreas sends insulin to convert the sugar into quick energy. Under these circumstances, you are stronger, faster, and smarter than usual.

You have no doubt heard stories of parents who were able to perform superhuman feats of strength and endurance when their children were in danger. The physiological reactions associated with fear made it possible. You have also heard of athletic teams that lost games because they became overconfident. Since they were not nervous, they did not have those physiological reactions and so were unable to do their best.

Of course, stage fright can be harmful. It can cause shaking muscles or a kind of paralysis of the brain. So it needs to be controlled and made usable. Here are six suggestions on how to do that.

1. *Recognize the positive attitude of your audience.*

You are nervous because you are something of a perfectionist, and you are making great demands on yourself. Your audience will not be that demanding. They will welcome the opportunity to hear you speak, and they will be eager to see you succeed. It has been my experience that audiences are wonderful. They forget the bad things and remember only the good things. Having spent much of my life in front of audiences, I have done just about every embarrassing or ridiculous thing that anyone could possibly do. I have sometimes been so embarrassed that I wished the stage would literally open up and swallow me. After some of these performances, I slipped quickly and quietly out the backstage door so that I wouldn't have to face my family and friends. But I found out later, in almost every case, that the audience either didn't notice or didn't remember what had happened to me on stage. This probably shows that what we do—good or bad—seems more important to us than to others. It also indicates that audiences are very positive in their attitudes and really want the performer to succeed.

2. *Prepare carefully.*

You will feel more confident if you know that you are in control of yourself and your material. If you're to make a speech, outline it and practice it until you know what you're going to say and how you're going to say it. Rehearse aloud to find out how your speech will sound. Rehearse before a mirror to see how your presentation will look. Practice before family and friends to get the feeling of an audience and to achieve a good, easy flow of words, movements, and gestures. The resulting feeling of control will greatly increase your confidence.

3. *Act poised.*

Don't be cocky or conceited, but act confident. Use a strong, firm voice, direct eye contact, alert posture, and positive movements and gestures to convince others that you are confident. If you do this, you'll convince yourself too. You may be putting up a front at first, but real confidence will develop quickly.

4. *Use vigorous physical actions.*

The adrenalin and blood pumping into your muscles demand action. In a fear situation, your whole body tells you to do one of two things: run, or stay and fight. When you make a speech, you can't do either. But you still have all that extra energy and strength to use up. If you don't use it, your muscles will stiffen and you may feel and even look "stiff as a board." Plan movements and gestures that will burn up excess energy. Visual aids give you an excellent opportunity to do this. Vigorous physical action not only helps you cope with your nervousness; it makes you more effective in your communication. You reinforce your vocal message with physical signals, and the vigor of your movements suggests that you are an enthusiastic person eager to communicate with the audience.

5. *Concentrate on your message and your audience.*

Uncontrolled nervousness is largely a result of worrying too much about ourselves. Characteristic thoughts are: "I wonder if *I* look all right"; "I wonder if *I* sound silly"; "I wonder what they think of *me*." The solution is to concentrate so hard on communicating what you want to say that you haven't time or energy left to worry about yourself. Try thinking of yourself as merely a medium, an instrument through which a significant message can be transmitted to an important audience.

When you select your topic in the first place, choose one that you think has genuine significance for your audience and specify in your own mind the reasons for its importance. When you give the talk, remember and re-create your original feeling of enthusiasm and your conviction that the material is important and valuable. Concentrate on how to put your message across to the audience, by selecting vivid words and examples that will communicate your ideas clearly and forcefully to your listeners. Keep looking at the audience, individually and collectively, searching their faces for clues that indicate whether they are getting the message or not. If they don't seem to be getting it, don't give up—try harder. Think of yourself as a philanthropist, not a failure: the audience *needs* to know what you are trying to tell them. Keep adjusting your material and your delivery to the response your audience gives you.

If your mind goes blank, don't panic. Just look at your notes; that's what you have them for. Don't be awkward or apologetic about it. Your audience doesn't care that you've forgotten. They just want to hear what you have to say. Look at your notes, casually and confidently, and then continue when you know what you want to say next.

If you can concentrate entirely on your message and your audience, you'll find that you can control your nervousness rather quickly and easily. You'll also find that your audience responds better because of your obvious eagerness to communicate with them.

6. *Speak as often as you can.*

Don't shy away from speaking situations. Seek them out. Volunteer to speak. Eddie Rickenbacker, World War I flying ace, volunteered to go on a lecture tour so that he could learn to control his stage fright. In this respect speaking is rather like swimming. The only way to control a fear of water is to get in and swim enough to develop confidence in your ability to stay afloat. The only way to control a fear of speaking before an audience is to speak enough times that you develop confidence in your ability to handle yourself, your material, your audience, and any problems that come up.

When the problems are unexpected, don't lose your sense of humor. If you can laugh at yourself, you can make a potentially awkward moment into an enjoyable one. "Mistakes" that the performer laughs at himself or herself are such a good technique for increasing rapport with the audience that many television comedians plan and rehearse several "accidents" for each show.

These suggestions are easier to make than to follow, of course. But if you practice (1) remembering that your audience really wants you to succeed, (2) preparing carefully for your speaking situations, (3) acting poised and confident in front of an audience, (4) using up excess energy with vigorous physical actions, (5) concentrating on your message and your audience instead of yourself, and (6) giving speeches as often as you can, then you will learn to control a fear that is difficult to live with and to develop the poise and confidence that can make you a more effective speaker and a happier person.

19
IMPROVING VOICE AND DICTION

An interesting voice is an important part of an interesting personality. The voice is the instrument with which we communicate. It is a highly individual instrument, as unique to a person as his or her fingerprints. Your voice can reveal your personality and character because it reflects your physical condition and emotional make-up. It can emphasize and illuminate what you communicate because it can so clearly show your feelings about the message you are sending. It can communicate, vividly and beautifully, a great variety of feelings: happiness, enthusiasm, sadness, conviction, sincerity, honesty, hate, tenderness, jealousy, and love.

The importance of voice in communication cannot be overemphasized, and the rewards for improving the voice are many. So it is important while you are working on improving your communication that you take inventory of your voice and formulate a plan for improving it. Ask yourself these questions:

1. *Is my voice too weak?*

Many people have voices that are simply too weak to express real conviction, vitality, or enthusiasm. These people often find at parties that they are unable to finish a sentence without being interrupted. It's not necessarily that other people are impolite and anxious to hog the conversation; it's just that a weak voice seems dull and uninteresting. You don't want to develop a big voice so that you can shout everyone down, of course, but you do need a powerful enough voice to make yourself heard without strain by all the people you are talking to. If you find it hard to project your voice with real vitality and conviction to the people at the back of your classroom, then you should do some work on developing vocal power. It will improve the quality of your voice even when you are speaking very softly.

The power source for your voice is the diaphragm, which is a group of muscles and tendons located between the chest cavity and the abdominal cavity. Most people fail to develop and use the diaphragm in breathing, and the result is a weak voice with a thin quality. If you are using your diaphragm properly, your upper abdomen will expand when you inhale and contract when you exhale. If your upper chest expands when you inhale and falls when you exhale, you're probably not using your diaphragm. Your breathing will be shallow, and it will not give adequate support to your voice.

To determine whether you are using your diaphragm and whether it is strong and flexible, try panting rapidly like a dog. You have to use your diaphragm to do that, since it is not possible with any other muscles. This exercise will let you see your diaphragm working and show you what it feels like to use it. To strengthen your diaphragm, try this panting exercise for a minute or two each day.

If your diaphragm is so undeveloped that you cannot do the panting exercise at first, you will need to do some preliminary exercises. Put your hands over your head with your arms close to your ears and reach for the ceiling. Stretch until you feel a pull on the muscles in your upper abdomen and lower back. Hold this position for a few seconds, relax, and then repeat the exercise. Do this a few times each day to strengthen the diaphragm. After two or three weeks, you should find that your diaphragm is strong enough for you to begin working on the panting exercise also.

After you have learned to inhale and exhale using the diaphragm, you should begin working on controlling the stream of air. To do this, take a deep breath, with the abdomen expanding as you inhale. Then purse your lips as if you were going to whistle, put your index finger in front of your lips, and blow a steady stream of air onto your finger. As you blow, the diaphragm should contract. Keep the steady stream of air going as long as you can. Repeat this exercise five or six times a day.

Another exercise you can use to learn to control the stream of air is counting, or reciting the alphabet. Once again, take a deep breath, expanding your upper abdomen as you inhale. Then, with the abdomen contracting as you speak, count as far as you can or recite as much of the alphabet as you can on one breath. Do this five or six times per day, increasing the numbers and letters as you go.

As you increase the strength and control of your diaphragm, you'll find that you are also increasing the quality and control of your voice.

2. *Does my voice have good quality?*

Many people have voices that are thin and colorless, or voices that become harsh as the volume is raised. Others have dull-sounding voices, produced too far back in the throat to have any brilliance or carrying power. Try cupping your hand behind your ear so that you can listen to the quality of your own voice. This is a technique that singers frequently use. If you have access to a tape recorder, record your own voice and listen to the quality. Here are some simple exercises you can use to improve the quality of your voice if you are not satisfied with the way it sounds.

The best technique you have for raising the quality of your voice is relaxation. If you can relax the parts of your vocal mechanism—your jaw, your tongue, your neck—then the important resonators—your mouth and head cavities—can do their job and you will get the best vocal tone possible. Massage the muscles in your jaw, throat, and neck gently, until they feel relaxed. Then let your lower jaw drop down and slightly back towards your neck. Be sure your jaw does not jut forward as it drops. Now, keeping your neck and jaw relaxed close your mouth and try humming parts of your favorite songs. You should feel the vibration of your voice on your lips and behind your nose in the mask of your face. When you can feel the vibration in both these places, your voice is correctly placed. Keep a steady stream of air coming from the diaphragm to hold the tone in these two resonating cavities.

Maintaining this same placement and relaxation, read aloud some poetry or sections from the Bible. When you do this, exaggerate the vowel sounds (a, e, i, o, u) slightly and feel the tone of these vowels in the two resonating cavities. The vowel sounds should all be open and voiced. These are the sounds that give beauty both to the language and to your voice.

Next, take some sections from your own speeches, underline the vowel sounds, and practice saying the sentences. This time don't elongate or exaggerate the vowel sounds, but pronounce them carefully and maintain the relaxation and tone placement that you achieved in the two previous exercises.

Don't get discouraged if improvement does not show immediately. If you continue practicing a few minutes each day, there will be noticeable improvement within a month or so.

3. Is my voice flexible?

A flat, dull monotone can make even an exciting subject seem uninteresting. A really effective speaker needs a voice that is capable of great variation in pitch (high to low), rate (fast to slow), and volume (loud to soft). The variations enhance the ideas being communicated and suggest a vital, enthusiastic personality. Listen to some people who really seem to enjoy life and notice the tremendous natural vitality that a flexible voice communicates. Then listen to your own voice, if possible on a tape recorder. Does it have the flexibility required to express a vital, enthusiastic personality? Is it varied enough to communicate the many shades and degrees of your feelings?

If not, here is an exercise that will help. From your favorite popular songs, select some that have especially meaningful and moving lyrics. Songs by the Beatles, Bob Dylan, Paul Simon, and Joni Mitchell might be suitable. Recite or read the lyrics aloud, with as much feeling as you can put into them. Concentrate on really feeling what the poet must have felt as he or she wrote. Try to express all the tenderness or bitterness, all the love or hate, all the anger or understanding in the song through the tones and inflections of your voice. Experiment with different pitches, different rates of speed, and different volumes. Exaggerate the variations at first, and notice how each change affects the emotion that you communicate. After you have experimented with all the possibilities you can think of, select the best pitch, rate, and volume for the lyrics. Polish your interpretation by varying the pitch, rate, and loudness to suit each verse, phrase, and even word, until your vocal tone and inflections communicate the exact feeling of the lyrics.

As you do this, apply what you have been working on in previous exercises. Support your voice with a solid column of air from the diaphragm and pronounce the vowel sounds carefully, with the tone placed forward in the resonating cavities of your mouth and head. Do this exercise every day, until you have trained your ear to demand variety and flexibility and trained your voice to produce this variety and flexibility easily.

4. Is my pronunciation accurate and clear?

Most of us tend to be lazy in the use of our lips and tongues when we speak. As a result we omit or distort many sounds, and our listeners may have to strain to understand what we have said. Notice the number of omissions and distortions in just one example: "Watcha gunna hafta do?" instead of "What are you going to have to do?" This lazy and inaccurate pronunciation often makes meanings unclear, interferes with vocal quality, and makes the speaker sound sluggish and lazy.

To find out if your tongue is responsive, say this: "Speak the speech I pray you as I pronounced it to you, trippingly on the tongue"—and say it trippingly on the tongue! Then try "She sells sea shells at the sea shore," with sharp, clear movements of the tongue to produce the repeated s and sh sounds. To check your lips, try "Peter Piper picked a peck of pickled peppers." If your tongue and lips do not respond quickly and easily, recite these and other tongue twisters daily, exaggerating the sounds made by movements of your tongue and lips.

Another good exercise is to say the following words, being careful to pronounce all the sounds:

literature (not litature)

candidate (not canidate)

accidentally (not accidently)

naturally (not *nachurly*)

realize (not *reelize*)

Now try pronouncing the following words, being sure not to *add* sounds that don't belong:

across (not *accrost*)

athletics (not *athuletics*)

drowned (not *drownded*)

attacked (not *attackted*)

barbarous (not *barbarious*)

mischievous (not *mischievious*)

As you rehearse speeches, for this course or later on, listen to yourself for clear, accurate pronunciation of the words you use. If you are not sure how to pronounce a word, look it up in the dictionary. Careful, accurate pronunciation will improve the quality of your voice, the precision of your communication, and the impression you make on your audience.

In this short chapter I have offered some simple, practical suggestions that can easily be used by anyone who wants to improve his or her voice for purposes of everyday communication. If you have serious problems in voice or pronunciation, or if you plan to enter a field in which your voice is especially important (such as acting, singing, radio or television announcing), you should by all means take specialized courses in voice and diction, vocal music, and so forth. But whether you take additional courses or simply apply the suggestions given here, remember that it takes a long time to make noticeable improvements, so don't get discouraged—keep at it. You'll be glad you did!